GW01316121

SPRITZER THE CAT'S AMAZING ADVENTURES

Dear Claire,
    Please enjoy reading my book.

Spritzer Abrahams

Copyright © 2018 Helena Abrahams

All rights reserved, including the right to reproduce this book, or portions thereof in any form. No part of this text may be reproduced, transmitted, downloaded, decompiled, reverse engineered, or stored, in any form or introduced into any information storage and retrieval system, in any form or by any means, whether electronic or mechanical without the express written permission of the author.

All references to a cat in this book are based on Spritzer Abrahams and her adventures. Any resemblance to any other cat or persons, living or dead, is purely coincidental.

This book is sold subject to the condition that it shall not, by way of trade or otherwise, be lent, hired or otherwise circulated without the publisher's prior consent in any form binding or cover other than that in which is it published and without a similar condition including this condition being imposed on the subsequent purchaser.

The views expressed in this work are solely those of the author and do not necessarily reflect the views of the publisher, and the publisher hereby disclaims any responsibility for them.

ISBN: 978-0-244-66583-8

PublishNation
www.publishnation.co.uk

ACKNOWLEDGEMENTS

Thank you to Marilyn Feingold for believing in me and helping my very dyslexic mum put this book together and encouraging her to go ahead with this amazing idea.

Thank you Sonja Mellish, for all your support when my mum wanted to throw the towel in and give up, and for helping with any computer issues.

Thank you Carl Roscoe, aka 'Tech Support', for all your help with all the tech issues and helping with all the finishing touches.

Thank you Gherkin, Mini-Moo, Bagel, Tinkerbella, Justice, Faith & The Crazy One Munchkin, who helped make this book possible with all their antics.

IN MEMORY OF MY SISTER GIZMO

INTRODUCTION TO SPRITZER

Spritzer came in to my life when I was asked to take her very young from a litter of kittens as the family were going on holiday. I always said at the time I would not be having any more cats, but after seeing her birth on video on Facebook live and watching her develop over her first few weeks of life, I knew I had to make her part of my cat family. She was always a feisty one as she managed to climb out of a very deep box on the way home in the car. She climbed all over me in the car – her first adventure. A cat with a social personality she immediately bonded with my alpha cat, Bagel.

Spritzer developed into a real character and followed me all over the house when Bagel went off to play.

She even got herself a role on a TV advert with myself, for a furniture company, which was shown as the Idents for Granada Weather, she beat many pets to win that role and when the day came for filming she filmed her parts in one take, she was very professional.

Of all my cats, as she got older, she tended to be the one who liked to wander away from the cottage for the longest time, she does live in cat heaven, surrounded by woodland and fields, so it was never a problem.

One day, Spritzer came back unwell, she was admitted to the vets and her stomach was full of objects, the vet had never seen this in a cat before, she had eaten, the mesh that goes around a joint of beef, a straw to drink from a can, and other items, we needed to know where she was getting these from as this was the second time she had done this. A tracker was discussed.

Totally out of character, Spritzer went out to play one day and never came home and one day led to nearly a week, posters went up all over Facebook, then one afternoon while the other cats were having their evening meal, Spritzer came trotting into the kitchen, very dirty and very hungry, she had clearly been trapped somewhere and was very happy to be home.

The tracker was ordered and I decided to start sharing Spritzer's adventures in blogs as I was surprised at how far she travelled and then I decided I wanted to get as many cats wearing the tracker as possible as there are too many cats that go missing, so Spritzer and her crazy adventures evolved.

REUNITED-VERY DUSTY,NO VOICE AND STARVING THANK YOU SO MUCH FOR ALL THE SHARES
This is Spritzer, missing since Friday 7th Oct, she is spayed and chipped, area Bury BL9.Fairfield Hospital Area Please check gardens, sheds, garages, outbuildings, quite nervous. Wearing collar and disc. Call day or night

 Write a comment...   Post

3

• 13 November 2016 •

Am I in bad books today!! oh yes...I woke mum up at 4.15am. Why? Because I can. Then when she checked up on my maps, she was less than pleased that I had ventured further into the hospital grounds and further away from the woods. So she was pecking my head for a good hour after I got in!!! Like I understand?... I only speak cat!! Now she keeps coming upstairs to try and change her bed, so I am refusing to budge, I am very comfy for now thank you very much. I intend to stay here until she feeds me again about four so for now Peeps, have a great afternoon
Spritzer Abrahams xx

• 21 November 2016 •

What a night last night, mum got no sleep as we all kept her up. I went off on my adventure and it was so cold I came back my usual way through the bedroom window. Never realising the tiles on the slanted roof would be covered in ice and I climbed, I slid back down, I climbed again, I slid back down, third time I threw myself at the window nearly giving her indoors a heart attack. Finally settled on mum's bed and Tink decided she needed to go out. Mum let her out and being a manic cat, she had to stay with her until she was ready to come back in. Once we all got ourselves comfy and back on the bed, there was the sound of someone sliding down the roof. Bagel, the big monster. It took him two goes of banging his collar tag on the window to be let in. By now mum was over going to bed to sleep.

Faith and Gherkin decided to have a game of chase around the cottage. Mum was now reading a book deciding, you get enough sleep when you die. But she is a grump today. We on the other hand all slept very peacefully on her bed. I think we have the best mum in the world. We have her so well trained. I was going to attempt to go out just now but the weather is so bad. I will just go and have a little rest with this tracker around my neck and catch you all later.

Purrs Spritzer Abrahams xx

5

• 23 November 2016 •

Woke mum up at 2.45am, I needed to go out and play. I managed a good 1.2km before I got back for breakfast at 6am. Tonight she has been making me pose on the stairs. I need new pictures for my new blog page. So I am sharing my new model shots with you all. She still has this tracker around my neck as you can see in the pics. I'm so used to it now. I still like to growl at her though when she puts it on me but that's just to remind her I'm the Boss!!!

Catch you all soon

Spritzer Abrahams xx

• 29 November 2016 •

Well as you can see the newbie arrived. Am I impressed? Not a bit!!! I will be teaching her who is boss when my mum's back is turned.

You can already tell though she is going to be an amazing hunter, she is a bit too good with her favourite mouse toy. Lucky I live in an area with plenty of mice to go around!!!

I decided to go on an adventure last night, I know how much she hates me venturing into the hospital, so I thought I would wind her indoors up and do just that!! I got the usual lecture today of "please stay in the woods, all that land and you want to go to the middle of the hospital". I just look at her and in my head I'm thinking, just feed me my breakfast slave!! (that's how all cat's see their owners)

I'm staying way up on my perch today away from Munchkin, she's like a kitten running on Ever Ready batteries. Catch you all soon.

Have a great day

Spritzer Abrahams xx

• 4 December 2016 •

Today I've been out playing in this fab weather. I hunted and killed and as a special treat for her indoors I got my tracker covered in all sorts for her to clean up. The way she was going on with herself, you would have thought I had brought my kill back for her!!!

I've even tolerated the newbie today, I allowed her to eat next to me without me growling at her. That does not mean we are friends yet. I will decide if and when we become friends!! I have my grumpy reputation to keep up!!

One good thing since newbie arrived, we all get an extra feed at night. That's the meal where she now puts the dreaded tracker back on me instead of chasing me around the cottage at stupid o' clock in the morning. Method in her madness!!
Signing off for now guys.
Spritzer Abrahams xx

• 8 December 2016 •

Yesterday I got another lecture for straying way into the hospital. All I wanted to do was eat my lunch in peace and she's down my ear going on with herself. I don't have a blinking clue what she's saying anyway. Not sure when she is going to realise that but I wish she would hurry up!!!

This morning I came back absolutely drowned from the rain, had my breakfast and decided I wanted to go straight back out again!! Well she refused to let me out without getting the tracker back on me. So then we had the dramas of the "chase" and after a lap of the cottage with her after me, with a raised voice, I was hooked up again and she let me go. Not sure why I bothered to be honest as she kept live tracking me. I was flashing like the illuminations, so I'm back home now sprawled out in mum's place on the couch, just to annoy her.

I'm going to get my beauty sleep then I will be recharged for my next adventure.
Purrs
Spritzer Abrahams xx

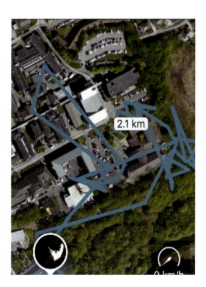

• 9 December 2016 •

Today I went on my second longest journey since I was fitted with this tracker, I came in at 4km. Why you ask? Because my mum went out at the crack of dawn for her hospital appointment and locked me out!!

As you can see from the different maps and mileage she was still keeping checks on me throughout the time she was away. I came back a couple of times but went off again as no point being hungry when I can go and hunt in the fields whilst I wait for her to feed me.

Finally, when she returned, way too late to call it lunch, it was after one and I was starving. I'm now beat and intending to sleep off all the mileage I have done today. So catch you all soon Peeps. Spritzer Abrahams xx

• 14 December 2016 •

So I woke mum up at 2am. She was not impressed at all. The tracker was already running but she needed to get me out from under her bed!!! I growl a lot, I'm one of those cats who is loving when I feel like it but can be a complete grump also. So she had to wait until I was at a point where she could grab me to get the tracker on.

It took her ages to coax me out and I put up a real struggle in her arms while she finally put me outside.

Clearly today, me being so late home and her doing a live check just as I was in the vicinity of the front door shows how in sync we are becoming with each other. But gosh, she looks rough today. I don't think the others let her sleep much last night, after I had played up, so she can't blame it all on me. But seriously the minute I come in the front door she starts going on with herself about how dirty the tracker is. Like I care? just feed me slave, (I mean mummy) I've built up a big appetite out on my adventures.
Eat/Sleep/Play that's my motto
Purrs everyone
Spritzer Abrahams xx

• 19 December 2016 •

So my mother, not even sure I should call her that, maybe, dirty stop out, came staggering in after 1am and tried to feed us all in a "I am totally sober kind of way". The packets of cat food she dropped on the floor, were just heavier than usual!! It's OK Mum we don't mind eating off the floor, as long as you don't make a habit of it!!!

I then thought I would really annoy her, I decided I wanted to go out but I didn't have my tracker on and I knew she was in no fit state to be chasing me. Or was she? O.M.G the chase was on!!!! Round and round the couch we went, she had trapped me in the lounge and I was growling and hissing like a lunatic but she does not fear me one bit and because of the drink she thought she was invincible. I didn't have a "CAT" in hells chance, she got me. The tracker was on and I was out on my backside.

I did the furthest journey this morning in the shortest time 2.6km in just 6 hours, I think I was running on mum's alcohol fumes. I'm off for a good rest now so catch you later peeps.
Spritzer Abrahams xx

• 20 December 2016 •

So yesterday she got this crazy guy in to fix these floating things to the wall. Could not for the life of me work out what they were for, even when Mum kept trying to entice me onto one of them. Every time she came into the kitchen she kept asking why I was still sleeping on the cupboard tops when the comfy hammocks were there for me?

Later when she came back from where she had been and finally saw me in one, she let out this high decibel shriek. I thought I was not meant to be in it and jumped out, little knowing that was her showing excitement I was using it.

So this morning when she saw I had obviously slept in one all night she just kind of shrugged but with a grin on her face.

I knew it would not be long before that blasted camera came out so here are my latest model shots for you all to see. I'm floating which is ironic as I'm the furthest thing from an angel you are ever likely to find!!
Well I'm off to have some late dinner peeps.
Spritzer Abrahams xx

13

• 23 December 2016 •

I woke mum up at 4.50am this morning banging the tracker on the shutters. Gave her a decent lie in for a change as I can be nice sometimes. When I got back at lunchtime though I was less than impressed to see my nemesis draped in my hammock. Miss Faith "NOT" snug as a bug in a rug. But "SMUG" as a bug in MY hammock!!! So I had to sleep in my basket on the floor as I had no intention of any confrontation that high up in the air.

Then the new addition I notice is stealing my thunder lately. Mum has that pink camera contraction aimed at her nearly as much as me now. I bet she has her own FB page soon. I am not impressed. The blinking rat was throwing herself at the fish tank this afternoon. Not sure she got the concept glass panel stops you actually attacking said fish.

Then her name disc arrived for her collar. If you have heard of Medallion Man, meet "Medallion Munchkin". It is massive on her. I heard mum tell her "she will grow into it" but for now it just hangs, looks nearly as big as her head. I'm off now to have my last little feed so mum can fit the tracker back on me.
Catch you all soon.
Spritzer Abrahams xx

14

• 24 December 2016 •

I travelled 2.1km this morning. I would call it more blown, the wind is that fierce around here, but I still got in serious trouble for going the deepest I have ever gone into the hospital grounds. Think she now regrets getting me banned from the mental health unit as I'm now having to find somewhere else to get spoilt. She is now talking about a camera as well as this tracker around my neck, to see what I'm up to. Is a cat to have no privacy?

At least I reclaimed my hammock today. Mum is buying more as everyone wants to be in them, but for now I will drape myself up here watching the world go by.

Spritzer Abrahams xx

• 1 January 2017 •

Hoping everyone had a Puuurfect New Year's Eve. I was out watching the fireworks. Blimey they know how to party around here.

I've been relaxing on my hammock most of the day, until Mum obviously just did a 24hr check on where I went last night and now she is making my ears bleed with her nagging. I'm now travelling way too far past the safety zone. I'm not sure at what point she will realise I only speak cat!!!

She got me banned from the mental health unit so as you can see I now travel round it instead of through it and I just happen to have found some houses I've not tried before but she thinks that is way too far to go on my adventures!!!

I'm trying to sleep Mum. Get down off the chair. Stop taking pictures, leave me in peace woman!!

OK peeps I will leave you all to recover from your festivities and catch you all very soon.
Purrs Spritzer Abrahams xx

• 20 January 2017 •

Hi peeps, not checked in for a few days. Her indoors has been that busy training the newbie to go outside on the lead, to get her off the cat litter completely. Now I am proud to say, at the ripe old age of nearly 16 weeks old she is out playing with no lead and completely toilet trained. She is only playing on the top garden up to now, but her tracker is being ordered next week. Going to be as big as her head!!! Don't think mum realises Munchkin is still only the size of a rat.

I have been travelling a fair distance round the hospital over the last two nights. I'm checking out hiding places for when the newbie starts following me. If she thinks she is getting the leftover food they give me at the restaurant, her and me are going to fall out!!! She can stick to eating the little flies she is loving chasing around the garden at the moment. I'm sure they will fill the little rat.

I'm now just lying in my hammock, yes, my hammock before my night time adventure. So I will catch you all very soon. Have a lovely weekend everyone.
Spritzer Abrahams

• 21 January 2017 •

I rocked in today absolutely filthy. I had been on the best hunt I had been on in ages. My tracker was absolutely full of gunk and didn't I know it. My poor ears have been ringing all afternoon.

She had to do a right good clean on not just the tracker, the collar too as that was also filthy. She clocked how dirty I was. You guessed it, she was chasing me round with that blinking camera to get pictures of my paws!!!

We all got spoilt with roast chicken tonight. So I'm just resting with a full tummy before I set off again wearing my shiny clean collar and tracker.

Let's see if I can get a little less grubby on my next adventure. Or maybe I could hunt, then have a quick wash at the riverside before coming home next time.
Night everyone.
Spritzer Abrahams

• 26 January 2017 •

Well today has been a really looooong day. The household has been up since 4am, when there was a very loud grating sound coming from outside the bedroom window. That grating sound was Justice doing a bit of ice skating on the frozen slates. He had got himself well and truly stuck on the roof and could not get to the window and didn't fancy sliding down the tiles. Poor Mum, up at stupid O'clock down the stairs, out in the freezing cold coaxing the ginger ninja off the roof. He ended up in the gutter piping. He is a big lad Justice; I am very surprised the gutter is actually still in one piece. Anyway after all that excitement we all got an early breakfast, so bonus.

I set off on a very cold adventure and took notice of the zillionth bent ear she gave me yesterday for travelling up to the maternity unit. She wants me to stay this end of the hospital, near the woods. Well she thinks I was listening. TRUTH, it was too blinking cold to travel too far from the cottage. I even let her give me a little love for about three minutes before I did my regulatory growl at her.

Can't decide yet if I am off out tonight or staying on mums bed. But will sign off now with a big PURR to everyone and show you my last few adventures.
Night night
Spritzer Abrahams

• 28 January 2017 •

Not been far today. I literally went out for less than an hour as the weather was so bad. But boy was I glad I did come back early. I had my lunch then got comfy in my hammock, then the entertainment began.

Mum needed to start getting ready for some "Do" tomorrow and needed to remove the old fake tan to put the new fake tan on. Well the bathroom is over the kitchen and the shower decided to leak through the kitchen. Munchkin decided it would be fun to skid back and forth through all the water on the floor, coming through the spotlight. I just sat there taking it all in knowing Miss O.C.D was going to throw the mother of all fits when she came downstairs. Boy was I right. Words unrepeatable on a cat blog were thrown about and I don't speak human so I have no idea what anything meant!!!

All I know was she went out and came back with something called a gun, I decided to stay out the way, I've heard about what they are capable of and some smelly stuff to seal the shower. Her and Munchkin were busy up there for quite a while but I believe the leak is fixed now.
Well I hope you are all having as fun a weekend as I am.
Spritzer Abrahams xx

• 1 February 2017 •

Hi Peeps, have I travelled today or have I travelled??

This morning Justice had us up at 2am crying at the window to come in. Then we all went back to sleep until 4.30am.

I went off on my first adventure at 5am. She starting telling me she needed me back by 10am but never said why and I never took much notice anyway to be fair.

I crossed the river on this journey into the far field and did 2km. When she looked back at the 24hr button she said I looked like I had been on acid, whatever that means.

When I got back, the dreaded cat carrier was there, so I sat high on my hammock refusing to come down, even when she tried to entice me with every product in the fridge. In the end she climbed on the chair and made out I was going to be given a whole packet of meat. So I jumped onto the fridge. She had lied though. She got hold of me and stuck me in the carrier. We were off to the vets for a Booster.

I won't fall for that again!!

I was in perfect health the vet said. I don't need anyone to tell me that. I'm Spritzer Abrahams.

I came back and had my lunch, then thought I'm going out again, and boy did I go on a long journey in a very quick time. 3.3km in a couple of hours and I've never been that way before. Way over the field I usually stay in and through a woodland I don't usually play in. So that's 5.3 km today.

GO ME!!
I'm shattered now. So having a little rest now.
Catch you all later.
Spritzer Abrahams

• 4 February 2017 •

Well the last two days I have done a 2.9km and a 1.9km adventure. Mum has been a bit sensitive so has been doing live checks more often. This thing around my neck has been flashing every five minutes. For my new friends that's the red lines on the pictures. This tracker makes sure us cats have absolutely no privacy whatsoever!! I was literally thirty seconds from the cottage today and there she was shouting me saying "come on Spritzer, I know you are by the garages" she was blinking right too.

I popped over the fence, she fed me and I went straight to bed. Munchkin the baby and all the others went out to play in the garden with mum as the weather was so nice today. I am just having a chilled weekend in my hammock. It was quite entertaining watching Bagel walk in after walking through all the mud up at the garages, where the path was being done, then happily walk all over her black floor & worktops. Her face was a picture. It was his turn for his ears to bleed with her going on with herself. I wouldn't mind, she is so good at cleaning up after us, if she just got on with cleaning up instead of going on with herself the job would get done so much faster.

Well I will wish you all a peaceful weekend and catch you soon.
Spritzer Abrahams

• 8 February 2017 •

Well I never usually get back early but am I glad I did today, it was like something from a carry on movie. Mum could not see one of the fish in the fish tank in the lounge and could not work out where it could have gone. She knew Bagel liked sitting up on the table watching them but had never known him to try and put his paw through the gap in the lid and didn't think devil kitten Munchkin had worked it out yet. The whole fish tank needed emptying to find the missing fish and that's no mean feat with a lunatic kitten at your ankles.

That kitten, within thirty minutes caused more chaos than a tornado in Oklahoma. She smashed mums favourite picture of her and her dad, while trying to help clean the accessories in the sink. Then she decided to tip the whole bowl of water over, that was waiting to go in the fish tank, all over the carpet because she just loves water and has to climb into it every chance she gets.

This kitten is really becoming the highlight of my day at the moment she is so blinking crazy.

So mum now has a big job on her hands clearing up, while I sit back and recover from my 2.1km adventure.
Have a great day Peeps
Spritzer Abrahams

• 9 February 2017 •

So today mum has had a blow heater on most of the day, trying to dry out the carpet where Munchkin decided to try and build an inside swimming pool in the lounge. I went out on my adventure managing 1.4km and when I got back there was a brown paper package in the sink that the devil kitten was trying to delve into before mum realised and put her on the floor. I later found out it was a parcel of new fish to fill the fish tank in the lounge. No interest to me. I was interested in the two packets of Purina on the table though. I rolled and snuggled the bags, showing mum how much I appreciated what she had bought us and then damn, I poked my blinking eye on the corner of the packaging!!!

What a prize idiot. In this house injured or ill cat means mum is on it like a car bonnet!!! I am now half blind trying to escape her clutches as she is trying to check me out. She finally catches me and after an assessment of said eye with me growling (for dramatic effect) she decides squeezing nice cold water in my eye will help cure me and it will open again. She wasn't wrong and after lots of growling (for even more dramatic effect) I can see again. I got an early feed out of it. So was all worth it!! OK, maybe not.

I'm now chilling in a very hot house as we await some dry carpets. I Suppose better hot than how cold it is outside now.
Catch you all later Peeps.
Spritzer Abrahams

• 15 February 2017 •

Well I hope you all had a Puuurfect Valentine's Day. Mum had Justice in the vets first thing as he was not his usual self. His tummy complaint had flared up so he is back on his steroids for a week. I had sneaked my way back into the mental health unit after weeks of being banished, blinking tracker, I can't keep anything a secret anymore!!!

I spent the day snuggled up asleep in the wardrobe and mum kept going on about having a date with Jim. We all waited with baited breath for our mum to go on her first date in over seven years and then she got in her gym kit!!! She had been winding us up all day. There was no Jim, it was Gym!!! And then last minute the lazy mare decided the Doritos looked more fun.

By 9.30pm the lot of us were all in bed. That doesn't work in this house someone's bladder always gives out and she has to get up and let someone out for one last pee-pee before sleep.

Only last night Munchkin got a second wind when Gherkin needed the loo and when she saw Justice in the garden, thought it would be a great idea to have a full on game of chase at 12.30am at night. All you could hear from the bedroom was mum shouting "Munchkin enough now!", "Munchkin, come here!" and "Munchkin, get down out the blinking tree!". I swear that kitten runs on Ever Ready batteries.

I've just got back from another journey via the mental health unit and today the house is peaceful. They are just putting the last few portraits up in our bedroom. Yes, folks we have our own bedroom. Spoilt or what???
Have a great day.
Spritzer Abrahams

• 17 February 2017 •

Well good afternoon everyone,

I'm in bad books.... Last night at 2.40am I had my mum chasing me around the lounge trying to get the tracker on and by 3am we were playing chase under her bed!!! Me growling like a complete lunatic and my mum less than impressed letting me know in no uncertain terms that I would not be leaving this cottage without it round my neck. She finally got hold of me on the window ledge. To be fair I was bored and just wanted to get out. I was sick of seeing her running round in her knickers. I got back for breakfast after going 1.3km.

Munchkin is now in training with her tracker, nothing fazes that head case.

I know mum is pretending to still be mad at me but I just caught her sneakily taking pics of me in my hammock. I intend to chill here now for the foreseeable, so catch you all later.
Spritzer Abrahams

• 22 February 2017 •

So I've just got back from a really wet adventure. My tracker was filthy, she had her usual moan, but nothing like her moan the other night when she stubbed her toe in the night when she was up for the umpteenth time letting one of us out and hit her little toe so hard it bled. I think they heard her in Australia. I think said toe may drop off, it is that badly injured, a bit like my poor ears from all the moaning!!!

Can you believe I'm even getting it in the ear with the rest of the gang for leaving dirty paw prints on her nice black floor? What does she expect? It's raining, we play out!! We run in! She forgot to put the towels down, now she has to mop again!! I say that's her own fault, we live with Miss O.C.D herself, we deserve a medal each.

I'm going to get my head down while my tracker recharges then I'm going out to get as dirty as I can and I'm going to come back and trash this lovely clean cottage, because I can!!!
Have a great day Peeps.
Spritzer Abrahams

• 25 February 2017 •

Well last night mum popped to the neighbours, sniffed a wine cork and was hammered. You know what that means? Yep, food everywhere, except in the food bowl, and her having to do a clean at stupid O'clock at night. Serves her right. She really is the worst drinker in history.

I decided to go out at midnight and when I got back at 6am everyone was already having breakfast. I knew mum would need to go back to bed and this morning I actually gave her loads of loves which is not like me at all, until we all crashed out again for another couple of hours.

After lunch I went for another sleep in the wardrobe but the blasted Munchkin found me and I spent about fifteen minutes playing tag from one wardrobe to the other. Really I just wanted to bop her on the head and tell her to go away, but she just has this way with us all.

My hungover monster, I mean mother, has just got me back in my tracker, as she finds it easier to get it on me in the day rather than chasing me round the cottage at night. So I'm resting up now ready for my adventure later.
Have a great weekend Peeps
Spritzer Abrahams

• 28 February 2017 •

So last night I went out on my usual adventure and managed 1.9km before at midnight the heavens opened with hail. I raced home, jumped on the slate roof and did exactly what I've chuckled at my brother Bagel doing before in icy weather. I slid down the tiles and ended up in the blinking gutter. Then bang, I knocked one of her new gutter spot lights off and it crashed to the floor below.

In for a penny, in for a pound, if I've made that much noise what's a bit more. When I finally made it up the tiled roof I then kept hitting the tracker on the window to usher her out of bed to get me out of the crazy weather.

While mum went downstairs to put the tracker on charge I just climbed on the bed and got myself comfy for the night.

Not sure how I managed it this morning but I escaped without my tracker on. Let me tell you peeps; I won't be trying that again. Two hours I was gone; you would have thought I was gone a week!! If you think I'm coming back to that ear bashing again you are very much mistaken. I think she forgets, it's her that has to put it on me, but it's my fault?? Lucky the weather was so bad, I never wanted to be outside. If she forgets again or is too busy, I'm just going to unplug it myself and carry it between my teeth!!!

This evening I've come in having done 1.8km. She tells me I stink of fresh kill. What a lovely welcome home, just as Justice is playing with a mouse in the garden. I think she's in for a long night, I'm off to bed.
Night Peeps.
Spritzer Abrahams

• 5 March 2017 •

Well what a few days it's been, Munchkin had her operation to remove her hernia and was also spayed and chipped. She has been put on cage rest for five whole days. It's like Christmas has arrived all over again. We can all walk around the house without her dive bombing us.

Mum has slept downstairs with her the whole time because although we all take the mickey out of her, she really is a good mum. I mean her on the couch means more room to stretch out on her bed. It doesn't get better than that really. The only problem with her being downstairs is, if you are out at night there is no way in until the morning as there is nobody to hear you bashing the window with the tracker. It only took me one night to work that one out though. People need to give us cats more credit, we really are quite clever.

So while I chill out here on her bed and she is kitten sitting downstairs, I wish you all a lovely Sunday
Spritzer Abrahams

• 6 March 2017 •

Last night I went on one of my mucky adventures, the tracker was absolutely filthy so out came the camera, I think you all know how she rolls now!! I did 2.9km and she did a live check on me (red line) for my new friends.

She let the rat, I mean Munchkin out the cage today, so the house is back to chaos. All us older cats running for our lives. She thinks she has to cling to everyone's necks as they pass her and hitch a ride.

It was quite funny though when mum never saw her and tipped a litter tray waiting to be cleaned, full of rain water all over her. (No litter in it) Then she really was a drowned rat. I thought mum was never going to forgive herself. Munchkin never even flinched.

This afternoon I left them all to it dismantling the dining room table that has been sold. Clearly seven cats helping, makes a job seven times harder. Throw lunatic kitten in the mix and I just heard "Munchkin, stop it, it's not a game, Munchkin, get off, Munchkin, where have you put that screw? Faith don't encourage her!!" Seriously peeps I live with this day in day out.
I'm just chilling now before I set off again tonight. So have a great evening everyone.
Spritzer Abrahams

• 14 March 2017 •

Been a few days since I wrote anything so I'm back to say hi ....and give an update of our crazy household.

Mum has sold the dining room table so we have loads of room at the moment to chase the red dot and watching the crazy kitten throwing herself all over the floor and up the wall is something not to be missed. I just sit in my hammock and take it all in and think she really is a grade one lunatic that Munchkin.

We all went to bed the other night and when we were all totally settled, Faith suddenly jumped up followed by Munchkin, then all hell broke loose!!! Mum had no idea what was going on as it was pitch black, the two of them started jumping up and down in the dark, doing some crazy kind of break dancing. Mum was trying to rescue all her breakable ornaments when she realised they were both after a moth. She finally found the light and Faith made one almighty jump, caught the moth and downed it in one. The two of them climbed back on mums bed and curled back in a ball and went back to sleep while Mum reorganised her shelf and herself!!!

Yesterday I did another Houdini act and escaped without my tracker, you know the next bit, ears bleed blah, blah, blah!! So today I did 1.3km and took a cracking picture when I got back, although I do say so myself. I'm now going for some well-deserved beauty sleep. So catch you all soon. Have a puuurfect day
Spritzer Abrahams

• 17 March 2017 •

OMG. I can't believe what I did at 4.30am!!! I jumped off the fridge and clipped mums gorgeous glass bowl and well you can guess the rest, it hit the tiles and smashed into a million, zillion pieces!!! I panicked that much with the noise I ran straight into the wall at the other end of the kitchen and landed in the water bowls and tipped them over.

You have never seen eight cats disappear so fast. Mum, well she was kind of calm, gutted, but calm for her. She looked at me with a look that said plenty without her having to say anything at all!! She just got on with clearing it up. It took her forever, there was glass everywhere and we were all just wanting something to eat but we didn't dare moan.

After the big clear up we were fed silently. So on a full stomach and a guilty conscience I went off on a 1.7km adventure but came back for lunch as the weather turned for the worse. She never removed my tracker as she has worked out I tend to trot off again now straight after lunch and I don't like to disappoint. So I thought I might go for one last run around before I have a rest for the afternoon. I did another 1.6km, but this time when I schmoozed up to her she removed my collar and as I went passed the cricket sounding toy, as annoying as it is I thought I would just give it a quick go and you know what, it's quite good fun.
Anyway I'm tired now as I've been up and about since 4.30am, so time for a snooze. So catch you all soon.
Spritzer Abrahams

• 26 March 2017 •

Hi Peeps, well with this fab weather I have been on a really long adventure of 3.1km last night. Her indoors, did a live check on me and could see me running back and forth in the woods, clearly on a hunt. Then I had a mad run right around the field.

I had to put a picture of my mum on today as it's Mother's Day. Happy Mother's Day to all you fab mums out there. Although mine is the best, paws down.

I have just had my lunch and now I am settling down for a rest.
Wishing everyone a Puuurfect day
Spritzer Abrahams

• 2 April 2017 •

Well what a fun thirty minutes it's just been in this cottage.

Mum decided to live track me and it was saying I was somewhere in the lane, but wasn't flashing red so she opened the front door to start calling me but I wasn't there. Munchkin kept trying to see what was going on. She isn't allowed out that way yet so Mum had to keep closing the door and moving her. Then when the tracker was checked again it was reading I was now around the back, so Mum went off to the back garden shouting me, knowing it is now a lot harder for me to get back that way as new neighbours have moved in with two dogs and they are using a section of land I use to get home, so it's all very difficult for us trying to adapt at the moment.

All I can hear is her shouting "Spritzer, Spritzer" Then she goes back to the front door shouting me again. I can hear in her voice she is getting more and more frustrated as she can see how close I am to home but can't find me on live track. She's now sitting in the garden waiting for a proper signal. Finally getting one, she can see I'm so close to the front door it's untrue, so she comes through to the kitchen again and attempts to call me, still no reply so she decides she better feed the rabble then go look for me. It's at that moment, the mention of lunch I decide to jump down off my hammock and let her know I've been watching her the whole time running from the front to the back looking for me and my collar has been flashing like mad all this time every time she has been live checking me. I snuck in ages ago, she never even thought to look up.

Well I've been entertained. Hope you all have a great day Peeps.
Spritzer Abrahams

• 8 April 2017 •

Hi Peeps, what a gorgeous day.

I went on a 2.7km adventure last night. I had to escape the madhouse, mum had been out shopping with grandma and came back with bags, and bags means places to play in for Gherkin who adores bags, but who had to get involved? Yep, the crazy kitten!!! It was all going off upstairs. Munchkin was dive bombing the bags with Gherkin inside them, Gherkin was getting angry but the Crazy One was relentless and refused to stop and it went on and on. Those Primark bags are top notch for cat toys UNTIL, that is, everyone is settled for the night and somehow the lunatic gets her head trapped in the handle, panics, runs under mums bed like lightning and it rips making the loudest noise ever. It only tears in half, so there is still half a bag being worn very nicely, though I say so myself, by a kitten, now running a million miles an hour around the house, trying to get it off with my mum running behind her in her undies, straight out into the back garden!!! I swear to god it's a laugh a minute since that lunatic arrived. At this point I decided it was time to make a short, sharp exit and leave them all to it, mum trying to catch Munchkin and everyone else sitting looking bewildered.

Have a great day in the sun Peeps

Spritzer Abrahams

• 13 April 2017 •

Hi Peeps, well it's been a week of tidying up after the flood in the cottage this week. I have tried to stay out the way as much as possible, even in the pouring rain yesterday I managed 4.8km but she wasn't impressed when I decided I wanted to eat on the hard tops instead of the floor for a change. It made it easier for her to remove my tracker, not sure why she had to moan.

Today the tracker has been flashing excessively She's been live tracking me so many times I think she's becoming the over protective mummy or a crazy stalker. I've not made my mind up yet.

There is just so much out there to hunt now, I'm having too much fun to just sit at home. I have a huge field and the woods all to myself to run back and forth across and play in. Only now "Big Brother" is always watching what I'm doing, but I know it's because she loves me.

I'm just resting up now before I venture off again but wanted to wish you all a Puuurrrfect Easter weekend.
Spritzer Abrahams

• 14 April 2017 •

Just a quick update to let you know I did a 2.8km journey last night. I just came back and mum removed my tracker to charge it so I could have my breakfast. Whilst I saw her talking to Justice I casually tried to sneak by her feet, to go straight back outside, to be swept up by her indoors and her saying "who do you think you are, Houdini? you don't go anywhere without your tracker, Mrs !!!" I'm thinking what the blazes are you on about? I only speak cat!!!

Anyway she managed to hold me whilst unplugging the tracker from the wall and attaching it to me. I'm already off on my second adventure of the day. I know she is live tracking me because it's dark in these bushes and I'm glowing like a Christmas tree every time she presses that button!!!
Happy Friday
Spritzer Abrahams

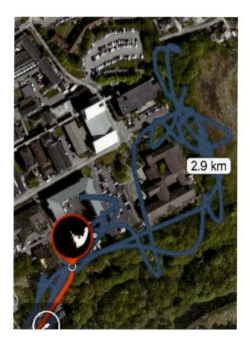

• 16 April 2017 •

Morning Peeps, I've been on one of my shorter adventures today with this horrid weather, only 1.7km clocked on the tracker. Come back and the Crazy One is running around like a lunatic so I have found myself prime position in my hammock to sit and watch her shenanigans.

So I will wish you all a very Happy Easter. Don't be eating too many eggs!! Mum has no eggs. She demolished hers Friday but keeps talking about some chocolate monster breaking in to the cottage and getting them. She wonders why we are all a little cuckoo, we wouldn't have her any other way and if she wants to believe in chocolate monsters we have decided to play along with her and watch out for the chocolate monsters!!!
Have a great day Peeps
Spritzer Abrahams

• 18 April 2017 •

I have had such fun today. There is soooo much work going on in the lane. So many garages open to investigate. I got home after a really good hunt and mum was not yet in. When she eventually decided to come home I greeted her at the door all loving for her to see my tracker covered in guts from my hunt, and going on with herself because my beautiful coat was covered in dust. Of course it was, myself and Bagel had been playing in the garages. She hadn't seen the state of him yet!!! His face was a picture, she likes us all perfect but we like to get down and dirty when we find somewhere to investigate. Well poor Bagel has been having his face wiped for the last ten minutes but the grime isn't shifting. He is such a character, one-minute running around with a squirrel in his mouth, the next, a big softy walking around on mum's hip like a baby. He is my favourite out the cat gang, we get on the best and now the summer is approaching we will spend more time having fun together. So today I'm letting you see a picture of the state Bagel's face is looking after playtime up at the garages. Yet again, my tracker is covered in guts which mum has now kindly cleaned up and is charging ready for my next adventure.

So catch you all soon I'm off for a good wash to clean all this dust off my coat.

Spritzer Abrahams

• 21 April 2017 •

Today I had a 3.7km adventure. I really did get about the hospital grounds. Mum went out and I still wasn't back when she got home, so the usual over protective mother kicked in. The tracker is flashing and if her indoors doesn't think her slightly hysterical voice can't be heard when she is shouting me from the front door of the cottage around the grounds of the hospital, she is very much mistaken. I hide under bushes to drown out the high decibels. Cats have very sensitive ears you know!! I'm wondering when she is going to realise this.

I cringed walking down the lane today with all the workmen outside. Her letting them know she knew exactly where I was. Explaining to them that I was too scared to come out because of them using the saw in the lane. Nicely of course, but god, I'm a big girl now, I'm sure I can get myself home. So I trotted down that lane like I was parading at some cat show. I was going to show her I could look after myself.

So as revenge for showing her I didn't need mummy's help, after my lunch she gave me my monthly dose of flea treatment. How I hate that. So I'm now having a sulk in my hammock.
Wishing you all a Puuuurrrfect weekend
Spritzer Abrahams

• 22 April 2017 •

Well what can I say? I was just out in one of my favourite play areas and who rocks up? My MUM!!!

I refused to move I just sat there talking back to her in cat, lucky she didn't have any idea what I was actually saying, I mean can't a cat play anymore?

Then her face was a picture when she realised Bagel was also with me. As I refused to move she thought I was injured so she started to make her way down the steep embankment. I thought at that point I better run. Didn't need her ending up in A and E for no reason.

I can now see her videoing me in the dark, something to do with showing all my lovely followers how easy it is to find a lost cat at night if they wear a tracker.

I think although not impressed where we both were. She felt a little more relaxed once she knew I was with Bagel. But to stand on the hospital car park shouting to us to please get home now at the very moment there is a nurse change over at the mental health unit nearby, she looks like she's talking to nobody, well enough said really.

So as she now knows about my own little adventure playground, I hope she doesn't make this a habit. I'm going to lose all my street cred around here.
Wishing you all a Puuurfect weekend
Spritzer Abrahams

UPDATED at 3.30am: Unbelievably it's after 3am and my mum yet again rocks up at the adventure playground. The look on her face tells me this time she means business and isn't going home without me!! I again take off to run and no amount of her calling me is going to make me go to her. I'm finding this fun now. Middle of the night she wants to be in my territory. She suddenly ups and leaves, I try to see where she goes but all I see are the car lights drive off. But five minute later she's back shaking the Dreamies and I'm already on the car park. After a few rolls on my head and eating a few Dreamies she finally catches me and blow me she's even got a cat carrier with her, she was never leaving without me this time.

Well after a good feed and removal of the tracker when I thought she was again going to be rushing me out to the vet, this time after the amount of blood all over it. I got a thorough examination only to be given the all clear.

The reason I obviously hadn't been home was I had caught myself some whopping big kill up there. But if she wants to come collecting me at this time every morning so I can climb in my hammock with my full tummy and go to sleep who am I to stop her?

• 24 April 2017 •

I came back early for my breakfast this morning and she was M.I.A again!!! My tracker was flashing away whilst I was banging at the door so she was checking on me yet again from wherever she was.

I didn't hang about, I decided to go straight back out to the big field and find my own breakfast.

When I arrived home the second time, just as I was about to bang at the door, which is what I honestly do everybody, she arrived to open it and the tracker was yet again flashing, so I'm guessing her mother hen instincts were kicking in and she was worrying where I was and she was so pleased to see me.
Have a great day Peeps
Spritzer Abrahams

• 26 April 2017 •

OK, so......I'm putting out an urgent call for everyone to help me find my mum a boyfriend!!! Or a life!!!! She's only gone and rocked up on another of my patches, shaking the Dreamies. Like I'm going to fall for that old chestnut again.

I've not been home for so long the tracker battery is about to die. I've not been back because the weather is finally good and I can finally have a great time in my tree and playing in my field, I just look at her and think, will you go home and clean and drive the other's mad, just leave me to my fun, and I will be back when I am good and ready!!

So folks until I decide I'm through with my adventure I will catch you all soon
Spritzer Abrahams

• 27 April 2017 •

So after another 3am where mum turned up and brought me home in the cat box because I had run the battery down again being out so long. I've stayed put all day. Actually call it grounded. Somehow mum had stopped the tracker from working on the App and there was no way she was letting me out until the problem was solved. It took most of the afternoon but finally the amazing lady from the customer service department worked out what had happened. Mum could not thank her enough as she knew trying to keep me in would have turned into a full blown nightmare. I am a free spirit and like to go off when I decide!!

But I have been patient and pretty content lying in my hammock all day in anticipation of getting my tracker back. She refitted it at my evening feed and has just taken a photo of me draped back in the hammock again. She has added me to Instagram recently and these photos and captions have got me more likes and followers than any others I have added and she is getting a little giddy every time I get another follower. So for anyone interested it's an Instagram address: @spritzerabrahams. She's about as proud as when I shot my TV advert a few years ago.

Well I'm almost as recharged as the tracker now so I will be updating you all very soon on my adventures.
Have a Puurrrfect evening Peeps
Spritzer Abrahams

47

• 6 May 2017 •

Well, I've just been on one of my quicker adventures but still managed 3.6km on my adventure today. I knocked on the door and everyone was still eating which never happens. I usually swan in late and eat on my own. As usual she had a moan because the tracker was covered in gunk and as usual I just looked at her over my bowl letting her know from the look I gave her. A) I only speak cat so have no clue what she is going on about and B) does she really have to waffle on while I am eating, it can cause indigestion?

I am disappointed in the weather today. All that lovely sunshine has gone. So I'm just going to be very lazy and from all the paint tins on the floor and sand paper, it appears I might just be getting a show of my own. I think she's going to attempt to tidy the ceiling where it's been plastered. That could be a fun update!!watch this space.

So for now Peeps have a Puuurfect weekend.

Spritzer Abrahams

• 8 May 2017 •

OMG If my mum is a full shilling then I'm not Spritzer Abrahams the adventurous cat!!! I've come in from my 4.2km adventure and had my breakfast, and she's finally decided to tackle the ceiling. Well firstly who wears nice clothes and boots to sand a ceiling? Only my mum!! She does cover the floor, kind of, with the cat towels. But within minutes the crazy kitten is skidding into them finding it all very amusing.

So as mum now starts changing colour in front of my eyes, from white woman to dust monster and moaning she is blind, because it's all got in her eyes, then spitting because she's talking and it's now in her mouth!! It's like a carry on film. Then she's down the ladder, the shutters are closed and I'm getting a full strip show!! Not only does my mum chase me in her underwear, she sands the ceiling wearing her undies as well!! It's all a bit confusing as her clothes are already trashed from where I'm chilling in my hammock. The kitchen looks like a sand storm has blown in from the Sahara but I know with her O.C.D everything will be back to normal asap.

So while I chill here chuckling to myself. I wish you all a great day Peeps.

Spritzer Abrahams

49

• 12 May 2017 •

Well Peeps, at 3.30am my mum yet again rocked up to my play area in the Mini. I shot off and sat in the tree in the pitch black listening to her calling me. I started to eventually chat back to her. When eventually after a while she worked out how to use the torch on her phone we sat having a two-way conversation, her trying to persuade me it was time to come home so she could charge the tracker, me telling her in cat to stop shining that damn light in my eyes, I could see perfectly well in the dark.

She kept turning her back on me pretending to walk off but I'm getting so used to this game now, I know she will never leave me. if she has made all this effort to come and find me at stupid O'clock at night, I will go when I am good and ready!!!

She keeps shaking the Dreamies and to be fair I have missed them the last few days being out on my adventures, so when I see her turn around to leave for about the tenth time, I jump out my tree and head off to the car park and walk towards her. Then as she bends to stroke me, I walk straight on by and roll over for effect in the middle of the car park and have her following me, trying to catch me. She drops some Dreamies and as I go to eat them she catches me and puts me in the cat basket and we head home. Everyone gets yet another very early breakfast thanks to "MOI" and after mum has put the tracker on charge I jump in my hammock and everyone including mum heads back to bed. I went many miles over the last couple of days but I ran the tracker flat playing out so long. So it has had all day charging. She has just put it back on me now for when I go off on my next adventure.
Catch you all soon.
Spritzer Abrahams

• 15 May 2017 •

Mum is not well today, so when I got back from my very short adventure of only 1.5km I went to sleep with her on her bed. Well it was not just me, there was the crazy kitten Munchkin, Gherkin, Faith and Bagel. Lucky it's a huge bed, she dragged herself out of bed to feed us all and then when her back was turned I decided I fancied a taste of the toast and jam she made herself!!

Blimey, she never even bothered with that screechy voice she uses when we annoy her, she just gave me one of those "REALLY Spritzer Abrahams? " looks. So I had one more really good lick of the jam, then watched as she tipped it all in the bin and started again!!

She really must be poorly. So off we all trotted back to bed for the rest of the day. We have all just had our Dreamies treats and I've had my tracker put back on. I'm hoping this weather improves soon as I'm getting a bit bored just lying around all day. Far more fun having mum come find me when I've been AWOL for a while. Wishing you all a Puuurrrfect week.
Spritzer Abrahams

• 21 May 2017 •

What a week!!! Mum has been falling to pieces with man flu!! Just when we thought she had turned a corner, she started with a nasty cold yesterday. So she is now sneezing all over us, which isn't pleasant, let me tell you. The Crazy One keeps diving inside her box of tissues that she is wandering around with, which is not going down well. I think she has blown her sense of humour out of her nose myself but I think it's quite funny.

She could though have lost her sense of humour when said little one got white paint on the black carpet, when mum thought it might be a good idea to try and tidy the woodwork for when the cottage goes for sale. You see the crazy kitten thinks she has to help with everything, so to get herself covered in paint, then to run upstairs was not what mum had in mind to put value on the cottage!!! I think it's a good job mum had a sore throat, she just does her glare and we know we are in bad books.

Today Mum was in sync with me again, she live tracked me just as I was near the garages and I heard her shouting me, only she went to the back garden and I decided I would like her to let me in at the front door. So I just sat and waited until she decided to let me in. The tracker showed I did 1.7km today and I've had a nice love off mum now I'm home and eaten lunch, and now I'm in my bed ready for a sleep.
So I'm wishing you all a Puuurrrfect Sunday.
Spritzer Abrahams

• 23 May 2017 •

I know it has been a terrible day for everyone with the bomb in Manchester last night and I want to say mum sat up watching it all night on the news and #manchesterwillrecover #manchesterwillstandtogether R.I.P to those taken so cruelly and speedy recovery to those injured.

On a lighter note, I will share that even being ill she still ended up out looking for me last night as I was late back and she wanted to check on me. I made her work to catch me. She was happily shouting me in the usual place, but with all the rain the weeds had grown so high, she could not see me although she could hear me talking back to her. This was going on a good twenty minutes and just as she thought she had me close two nurses approached me and I bolted. I could hear the nurses talking to my mum through the bushes. They showed her a way through to the side I had been on. She couldn't believe she has just spent twenty minutes shouting through bushes and scrub when she could have walked five minutes round the other way and been able to see me. Anyway, she knew now for next time. I had bolted down the side of the mental health unit and she was busy showing them the tracker. She couldn't get me to come back to her so I saw her drive off. She must have looked at the App, though on her phone and seen I had headed back up to where she had been and turned back to find me. This was so much fun.

Next minute, she has parked up again and is now following me around the unit, calling me but I'm not quite ready yet to go home!! So she goes and sits on a wall. Now, I'm nearly ready. I climb the embankment and that's when the video starts rolling. So I perform for her. I'm such a diva. We have now been playing chase for a good hour. so I finally let her pick me up and for the first time ever there is no cat basket. I'm loose in the car. I sat on the back window ledge like the princess I am until we got home. I had my dinner then climbed in my hammock for a lovely cat nap.
Spritzer Abrahams

• 28 May 2017 •

So it's a long weekend. I decide to come home after going AWOL for nearly three days. Mum seemed really relieved. She is still not properly better, so my ears did not bleed that bad this time. She can't speak for that long before her chest hurts so whatever she is babbling at me, was for a much shorter time than usual!! I had the best time on my adventure, the sun was shining and I brought her back lots of evidence of my hunting all over my tracker.

We all got the most amazing cooked chicken last night, she fed me like the princess I am in my cat bed, her on her knees, one piece at a time. I don't have to ever move once I get home; she truly is my slave!!! The crazy kitten on the other hand has been driving us all doolally, she is obsessed with catching flies and wasps. YES, wasps and then it's a full on mission chasing her around the cottage to get them out her mouth, what a lunatic!! The one's mum misses are all over the floor doing a form of backstroke as they can no longer fly!! When she isn't on a mission to kill every flying thing, she has to wake up Justice. The poor boy wants two minutes sleep, and she thinks everything is a game, everything is there to be dived on!!

Today I went on a 2.2km journey. I came back early this morning as it was raining and I'm just chilling out today in the large cat basket. Mum is tanning a nice shade of orange in her onesie, her usual Sunday ritual.

She was not happy this morning when crazy kitten was running in and out and getting very angry with herself, until mum followed her outside and found a nice big rat as a gift. Justice most likely caught it, but it could have been Bagel. The kitten just wanted it shifting away from where she wanted to pee. Mum did her duty, and after the mini tantrum, the Crazy One went and peed on the other side of the path on the soil there!! Yet again the slave did as she was ordered!!

It's been a quiet afternoon since that drama.

So I wish you all a Puuurrrfect rest of the day and great Bank Holiday.

Spritzer Abrahams

• 5 June 2017 •

Well I'm just seven years old now and blimey it's been a funny day. I came back really early having done 2.3km on my adventure. I had to get back quickly, as it was throwing it down. I ran upstairs, as mum was lying in bed, she had been up with the others since 4am. I jumped straight on the lovely clean bed, oh boy! Silly me, I never wiped my dirty paws on the way in and someone, no names mentioned had decided to put cream coloured bedding on when the forecast was rain all week!! Somehow that was "MY FAULT" and now, the bedding had designer footprints all over it. Never have I seen anything but black bedding in seven years, what is wrong with the woman??

After that episode was over, her indoors thought the woodwork could do with painting. I was just going to watch from the bedroom as it was obviously going to end in disaster!! She was happily painting away and all was going very smoothly until she saw the TV saying it was going to turn itself off in so many seconds. She grabbed the remote, covering it in paint, then in her haste to get to the bathroom to clean it up she swung her hair and it hit the doorframe. Well you can imagine the rest, she now had the most amazing white long streaks in her newly bobbed hair, but she was totally freaking out!! Her arm had now got covered and that had touched her favourite My Little Pony t-shirt. Well us cats may not understand humans but it was very amusing. She had soap on her hands, up her arms and now as she knew it removed paint she was washing her newly streaked hair in it!! The door went and she had to go and answer it with half a wet head of hair. it was her Asda delivery. He asked if she had been caught in the downpour. She explained she had been painting!! He just gave her a very strange look whilst nodding his head. The more I think about it, all us crazy cats were meant to find my mum when we were kittens, as we all have the crazy gene and to be honest I couldn't have wished for a better mum.

She has just given me my evening Dreamies and put my tracker back on for my night time adventure.

So catch you all soon.

Spritzer Abrahams

• 9 June 2017 •

So the last few days myself and the cat gang have just really been high on paint fumes, she is on a mission to get the cottage ready to go for sale. I love the way she escapes for a swim each evening while we all just sit in the smell bouncing off the newly painted walls!! I'm now a tuxedo cat with a white stripe across my back, which I refuse to let her brush out. I can be a right grumpy cat at times. I even sliced her hand the other night because she insisted on disturbing my beauty sleep to fasten the tracker on me, instead of waiting until I got up to eat. It's not bad enough she is constantly taking my photo at the moment, as in her words "there are some exciting things hopefully coming up in the pipeline".

She was AWOL when I got back from my adventure today, I was absolutely starving. I had to wait over an hour before she got home and fed me. I will let her off this once as she was seeing her amazing surgeon who got her walking again and gave her, her life back. Without that surgeon me and mum would not be having these crazy adventures together now. Her out searching for me at stupid O'clock, me driving her mad with worry when I'm late home.

Well she has just put the tracker back on me and I'm all ready for my next adventure.
Wishing you all a Puuurrrfect weekend.
Spritzer Abrahams

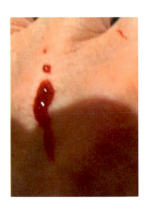

• 12 June 2017 •

Well what a night last night. I thought I would have a change and stay at home seeing as I was perfectly comfy, slap, bang in the middle of mums bed. What a stupid idea that turned out to be!!

Firstly, mum disturbed me by climbing in to bed, then she kept chuntering under her breath about having to be in the star position. I mean I was in bed first does that count for nothing??

Then the real fun and games started. Bagel has somehow managed to be locked in the house, so just as we all finally nodded off to sleep, he started playing with the shutters in the bedroom, so mum, trying not to disturb me too much hoisted herself up against the headboard, hitting her head on the overhang of wood. I pretended not to notice but had a little chuckle to myself before trying to get back off to sleep. She tried to get in to bed again without bothering me but I gave her a little growl to let her know I was not impressed. Off to sleep we went again when bang, chink, bang, chink and lots of crying at the window!!! You have got to be joking?? Now it was Faith wanting to get in at 2am and she was not going to quit tapping her collar disc on the glass!! Again, mum climbed up the headboard trying not to disturb me, like Faith had not already done so.

I now remember why I go out on night adventures.!! Mum spends all night being concierge and nobody gets any sleep in this cottage.

Thankfully we had an early breakfast and the tracker was already good to go from the previous evening. So the minute I had eaten I was OFF!! I only did 1.3km as I was absolutely shattered.

I have spent the day catching up on my sleep and tonight I am going back to night adventures.
Spritzer Abrahams

• 13 June 2017 •

Finally, a beautiful day for me to get out on a proper adventure. I have been running around the hospital grounds all day having so much fun. 2.7km on my adventure today. Just me, myself and I.

I know when I'm out all day mum is constantly checking up on me even when she has her own things to be doing. My tracker flashes every few hours, I could even hear her shouting my name earlier on this evening when she was going off swimming but I was not ready to come back, so I left where she knew I was playing and shot off back to my field. It is now officially my field. I have decided to stake claim to it, after playing in it for so long. I have the whole field all to myself to run around in.

Later on tonight, I again teased mum I was almost home, she went to the front door shouting me and when she realised I was not coming back at that point, closed the door. Next thing, she heard her usual knock of a cat tag banging on the door. Presuming it was me, she opened it to find the crazy kitten practically standing upright on her back legs, very upset at having been locked out. That did worry mum as she had not seen how she had got out, so was trying to work out if the Crazy One had learnt to finally climb the fence at the back and cut through the woods, go behind the garages and come back down the lane. I think this now means the Munchkin's tracker is ready to be worn fulltime. Finally, she just did one last check before bedtime and saw how close I was, so thought she would call me one last time. I love the fact she was still up, as it meant I got my dinner when I got back but she needs to stop standing in the middle of the lane in her pyjamas and a wet towel on her head shouting my name. It's not the best look in the world.

I'm all snuggled up now on the couch. Just been told mum has been in touch with the company I did my TV advert for and is trying to get a copy to share on my blog.
Just call me diva cat, only joking. I'm just little old me.
Night All.
Spritzer Abrahams

• 15 June 2017 •

I went on a 24-hour adventure. Came back just in time for my lunch today. Clocked 2.3km on my adventure. I've had a really lazy day sleeping on mums bed. She had to finish a few chores and was moaning her body was aching from said chores and cleaning three fish tanks.

But tonight she has excelled herself. We stink, yes, I said stink!!! She has never cooked in forty-six years and for some random reason known only to herself she felt the need to try and cook real chips tonight??!! She fogged Faith out the hammock in the kitchen within ten minutes. She was flapping the tea towel over the fire alarm just to prevent it going off. The chicken pieces to go with these chips ended up being charcoal chicken as they cooked too quickly in the oven. She never has mastered the technique of having two things ready at the same time!!! Eventually she realises the chips needed the heat turning up to give them a fair chance of cooking before sunrise. Then her best move of the whole cooking experience. Put the wok in the oven while she eats her dinner so no cats burn themselves!!! REALLY MUM?? didn't you use the oven to cook the chicken?

Well she moved like grease lightning at the smell of au d' plastic melted handle!!

The scent around the cottage this evening is shall I say, different. She has a candle lit now to disguise all the cooking/melting scents of earlier on. I was feeling quite recharged before she fumigated the property, now I need a little more time to find my legs again and I will be out of here for some fresh air.
Catch you all soon peeps.
Spritzer Abrahams

• 21 June 2017 •

What can I say.... I've just been carried home by my mum, I've no idea what all the fuss is about myself, but I believe the Oxford Dictionary is updating the meaning of neurotic to include the definition Heléna Abrahams when her beloved Spritzer Abrahams goes on an adventure and she somehow forgets to put the tracker on!!! I am only nearly four days' late home, what is her problem?? She forgot, it's not as if it's my fault!!! Anyway, I believe she has been a manic head looking everywhere for me these last few days, even going out through the night to my usual hang outs, but to no avail. I've been on an even bigger adventure, but because dippy head forgot to switch on the tracker we have no log of distance.

I have covered many km, and now as I was just very deep in the woods I heard a very hysterical voice shouting my name. I thought I would let her call out for a while, shocked she had found me this far in to the woods, so I just watched from my hiding position, then when I saw she was about to give up and go home I popped up and meowed back. Wowzer, was she elated to see me, I decided to chat from my spot for a while, then as she started walking I decided to run down the hill to join her and give her lots of loving. She put the tracker button to on so quickly and carried me home like the princess I am and I got two pouches of food I was so hungry.
I am now snuggled up on mums bed. I really need some sleep and so does mum from the looks of her.
So catch you all soon.
Spritzer Abrahams

• 22 June 2017 •

Well today has definitely not turned out the way I expected. I came back from my night time adventure clocking 2.2km on my adventure and it was great to get some loves from my grandpa who was visiting, he spoils us all. He was very worried when I went missing but he knew I would be back.

Mum put my tracker on charge so I now have to wear Munchkins until mine is charged just in case I run off again.

But I took poorly this afternoon. I have had to visit the vet. I have eaten something that must have been a bit off while on my adventure and ended up with a poorly tummy. I am now on horrible medication for the next five days. That will teach me to go hunting.

I am feeling very sorry for myself this evening and when I try and sit downstairs she keeps putting a towel under me so I'm going to go and sneak upstairs now and sleep on her bed while she is making herself something to eat.
Hope you all have a lovely evening.
Spritzer Abrahams

• 23 June 2017 •

I'm still feeling unwell today, but I am back in my own tracker now. Last night I just lay in mum's room feeling very sorry for myself but she did keep coming and checking up on me. When I started growling she knew it was time to leave me alone.

Then the time came for my dreaded medicine, that's when I turned into Psycho cat. She tried so hard to get that paste and tablet down my throat, even wrapped me in a towel but I escaped, so she then tried it in food. Does she really think I got off the banana boat? ONE - NIL to Spritzer Abrahams

This morning at breakfast as I was eating away she grabbed me from behind and it all happened so fast, mouth open, tablet down throat, paste injected in, that is ONE - ALL.

I have spent the day sleeping on the couch next to mum and the vet says tomorrow I should be much better. I hope so.
Catch you all soon-have a Puuurrfect evening.
Spritzer Abrahams

• 25 June 2017 •

Hi everyone, I'm feeling so much better today. Thank you so much for all the get well wishes. I went out for the first time yesterday, but took it easy and only did 1.2km, but last night I was back to going out again on big adventures and clocked 2.9km, can't say I learnt my lesson about not hunting as I've just got back smelling of fresh kill, mum was down my ear letting me how I had not even finished my medication yet, even Munchkin came to sniff me. I just cannot help myself!! I love to hunt.

I've got to tell you though, the fun never stopped in the madhouse whilst I was ill. She is still getting the cottage ready for sale and decided it was time to paint the loft hatch, which meant it would have to be kept left open all day. Which meant every time she needed to get to the bathroom she had to crawl down the corridor, on her hands and knees, pretty amusing for the cat gang to watch let me tell you. Only it got to bedtime and the gloss had not dried to close it. So off to bed we all went.

At stupid O'clock am, when the crazy kitten decided it was time for an early breakfast and mum was still not awake properly she got up and YES FOLKS-YOU GUESSED IT- she walked straight into the open hatch. The cats who were still sleeping were now wide awake trying to escape what they thought was an intruder in the house, while mum sat on the floor saying words I cannot repeat, and as for Munchkin, she just sat with mum crying for food. Didn't go down too well, let me tell you.

I'm thinking it's time for her to quit with the DIY, she messes up every time!!

I'm going to have a chilled out day today in my hammock, as the weather is so bad now, so have a Puuurrfect Sunday.
Spritzer Abrahams

• 27 June 2017 •

I clocked 1.5km on my adventure this morning. This weather is seriously bad for me trying to have fun outdoors. I just keep getting wet through and ending up stuck at home all day. At the minute being at home is pretty lethal, good job us cats are insured, I think maybe it's time mum thought about getting herself insured!!

I'm thinking about changing her name to Bob the Builder. I came downstairs yesterday afternoon to find everything from under the kitchen sink cupboard all over the kitchen floor and her trying to fit inside the cupboard cursing like a bloke, trying to fit a pipe back onto the bottom of the sink. Did she manage to fix it? did she heck!! Everything that was on the floor is now in plastic bags and there is a big bowl under the pipe work collecting drops, waiting for the plumber, who is booked for 10am tomorrow morning, and the crack she gave herself on the head getting out of said cupboard, well that's another story!!

I'm sure if she hits her head one more time this week, I'm thinking concussion maybe on the cards, or with a bit of luck the next bump on the head may knock some sense into her!!

But maybe I speak too soon. As I type this she appears with very tall ladders borrowed off the neighbour. What the heck is she planning next on her to do list? This causes me much worry. Thankfully they are just resting against the wall tonight so there will be no injuries this evening.

But oh god!! The wok has just come out again with the melted handle. Cat gang evacuate the cottage Noooooow!!!!! Said in my loudest cat voice.

Must go folks might need to limber up for a quick adventure. Have a Puuurrrfect evening.
Spritzer Abrahams

• 28 June 2017 •

I have just got in, absolutely drowned to such an ear bashing. I escaped a few hours ago without my tracker on. OMG are my poor ears feeling it now!! I found it quite amusing, her chasing me in slow motion, thinking that might actually make me stop and let her put it on me before I went out. I was like a ninja warrior the way I ducked and dived between the tables and couch, then out in to the garden before she gave up the chase.

What I don't understand is I get the ear bashings and last night after an hour of Munchkin not appearing, mum knew instinctively she would be on the other side of the high fence and so went to call her back. The crazy kitten just sat on the other side of said fence meowing back every time mum told her she would have to jump back over the same way she went. When it started to become apparent the Crazy One would be happy to just sit on the opposite side all night and chat to mum, what did she do? she relented to a scrawny kitten and lifted up the fence panel so the spoilt one could leisurely stroll back through!!! I mean really, this is pushing the word concierge to new limits.

Then this morning after feeding Mini-moo and praising her for managing to eat nearly all her food, she then went on to honk the whole lot up all over her set of keys, fur ball included. Talk about unfair, I never heard her raise her voice to her, she just donned the rubber gloves and went on to clear up said mess. OK, she did utter a few words under her breath!!

So I guess the answer is NEVER try and venture out again without the tracker on, I have got some revenge though, I am so filthy there is no way Miss O.C.D will be leaving that kitchen floor in the state my dirty paws have just left it.
I'm off to dry off.
Spritzer Abrahams

• 1 July 2017 •

I've spent the whole afternoon playing outside today. I've clocked 2.9km on my adventure. I have played in "MY" field and was having loads of fun. I'm not going to say my tracker was not on live track but every few hours I was flashing so much today. I'm surprised she didn't run the battery flat.

When the rain started I decided to go and visit a few patients in the mental health unit but because I am stalked by my mother I'm sure she will be putting a stop to that tomorrow!!

It was 9pm when I was hanging out near the nursery area, knowing she would soon be checking where I was and boy was I right 9.03pm the high pitched sound of my name being shrieked to call me home rang out.

I was met on the lane by Munchkin, Justice and someone who sounded like my mum but who was the wrong colour to be my mum. She could definitely pass as Justices mum because he is orange. What has she done to herself while I had been out playing today? she was tangoed!! but she has no shame, she stands in the lane shrieking my name, while tangoed and dressed in a onesie covered in penguins!!!

While she makes me some dinner I have a good sniff of the orange feet to make sure this is my mum and not some imposter, but once my bowl has been put down and the camera comes out I know for sure it's her. She never stops sticking that camera in my face, so tonight I felt like I wanted to stick my tongue out at her. Only she loved it and wanted more so I have snuck off upstairs to her bed. On the way I noticed the fake tan bottle waiting to go in the recycle bin. Funny thing is it takes a few days to fade, so if anyone sees an orange woman in Bury that is my mum.
Enjoy the rest of your weekend Peeps.
Spritzer Abrahams

• 3 July 2017 •

I came back this morning after clocking1.8km on my adventure. I was absolutely wet through and had to get mum out of bed as she had one of her dreaded migraines, but I needed my breakfast, so being the wonderful mum she is she never complained, no, she grabbed the blasted camera and started taking pictures of me because she thought I looked cute, wet to the bone!!! I only wanted my breakfast!!! Then when someone knocked at the door and the parcel she had been waiting for arrived, even my eyes lit up. Mine, because I saw a box to play with, hers because the canvas of the two of us had finally arrived. It's already up on the wall and looks "F.A.B" whatever that means, her words not mine.

This afternoon we are all having a bit of a pyjama party in mum's room as she needs to be in the dark. She's moaning a bit that we have a beautiful double bedroom of our own, so why are we all over her bed? But not speaking human we clearly can't reply and are going to just stay put. Gherkin is sleeping in her usual crazy position. I have given mum some foot space today. Justice has given up and gone on the floor and the crazy kitten is under the duvet. Why? I've no idea, but that's where she likes to be!!

Must get a bit of a sleep now before I go off on my next adventure tonight. I need my beauty sleep now my mum insists on taking all these pictures of me.
Spritzer Abrahams

• 5 July 2017 •

Well I became a total diva last night and decided I didn't want my tracker put on when my mum wanted to put it on, so it became a stand off!! Chasing me around the cottage, up and down the stairs, around the couch, trying to coax me out from under the bed with lots of treats. Then when she thought she had me cornered in the wardrobe, I growled, she flinched and I ran back downstairs and hid under the clothes horse. I find she uses these strange words when we get in these chases I can't spell these words, so I won't put them on my blog. She did eventually get the tracker fastened back on me, so she felt she had won, I was just full from all the treats I had eaten. She had not really won at all!!

I had to go and work off all the treats so I went on a 2.4km adventure today and when I came back the tracker needed a good clean as I left it covered in blood from what I managed to catch while out playing!!!! Call it more hunting. There was another new toy for me to try out when I had had my lunch, I did have a quick go but I really just needed my sleep.

She has just had a quiet word in my ear, telling me she doesn't want a repeat of last night. Obviously only speaking cat I have no idea what she means and can't promise her anything....
So I will wish you all a Puuurrrfect evening.
Spritzer Abrahams

• 8 July 2017 •

Hi Peeps, hope you are all having a lovely weekend, I went off yesterday and came back this morning clocking 3.9km on my adventure. I'm always so spoilt when I have been AWOL for a period of time, it's great, she soon forgets what a grump I can be.

I have to share what just happened while I watched from up high in my hammock. It could only happen to my mum aka Bridget Jones. She was happily collecting all the dry washing off the clothes horse, the front door was open as the weather is so nice today, she carried the pile of clothes upstairs. The postman knocked at the door as something needed signing for. She is shouting away upstairs "wait a minute, be with you in a minute" She finally comes downstairs, slightly pink faced. The postman is trying to keep a straight face while looking at something on the floor. Mum finally looks back to see what he is looking at, OMG a pink pair of her knickers are lying there in the middle of the floor, instead of just letting it go she starts making up excuses, "they fell off the pile of washing," she says, "that I had taken upstairs", while going totally beetroot in the face he looks like he totally doesn't believe her and probably thinks there is a bloke upstairs!!! I'm lying in my hammock next to Faith totally loving this, if we could high five we would, but we can't so we just keep watching her digging herself a little deeper into a hole. Think the postie was loving it too!! Bet it's the first time he won't be moaning about working on a Saturday!!

My mum on the other hand is talking about going into hibernation for a while, not sure what that means but sounds like my life would be pretty boring if she did that.

Now the knickers drama is over and the postman is gone we are all settling back down for an afternoon sleep and leaving mum to put the clean washing away.

Speak Soon Peeps.

Spritzer Abrahams

• 12 July 2017 •

I came back from a 2km adventure this morning to another earful. I mean this tracker goes beyond imposing on my privacy!!! She caught me visiting my friends in the mental health unit early this morning and now my poor ears have been bleeding listening to how I could have been trapped in the building, and the stress that would cause her having to look for me if the battery were to run out, etc. etc. etc..... I think I might actually enjoy the peace and quiet to be honest.

But then again if I were to be trapped, think of the things I might miss, like her dropping the dry cat food all over the kitchen floor like last night. Now that from my high up vantage point was very funny. She again used those words I can't repeat on my blogs!! She got on her hands and knees and picked every last one up by hand before remembering she had a dustpan and brush.

Today after taking the twins Faith and Justice for their boosters, when the baskets went back in the loft and the ladders came out I just knew that meant trouble. What was she up to now? Changing bulbs, OK. sounded easy enough, but this was my mum right?? What idiot grabs a light bulb that has been on for the last few hours to check the voltage of the new bulb going in is correct?? My mum now has a very red tipped finger, as said bulb was very hot!!! It's amazing to think she has survived this long on her own. I'm now staying out the way until the ladders go back in the loft. Catch you all later.
Spritzer Abrahams

• 13 July 2017 •

So today I clocked 2.6km on my adventure. I was on my best behaviour and never went anywhere I wasn't meant to go. I couldn't be doing with another ear bashing; they are still tingling from yesterday. She was kind enough to greet me in the lane, though she is becoming a little obsessed with her video camera if I do say so myself!!

She went out in the car after lunch and when she came back, she let out a scream that could be heard around the hospital grounds. The car door had smashed on her arm. It is quite funny to see her both laugh and cry at the same time. She always goes on about how good she is at multi-tasking, she can even do it with her emotions. After that drama ended all we heard was what a huge bruise was going to develop by the end of the day. Seriously, did she really think any of us were listening? Just get that oversized plaster on mum, that you really don't need!!! What did she do next? She got her DIY screw driver kit out. That could only mean trouble today and yep it cost her dear!!! She only went and screwed the handle too tightly on her hand made glass fronted drawers in her bedroom and the next minute the sound of cracking ice, no mum, that's the glass cracking, you numpty!!

I've added the email she has sent to a glazier company for a quote for a new piece of glass. I know she's a little dippy but I'm still glad she is my mum.

Well I hope you all have a Puuurfect evening.
Spritzer Abrahams

No Subject
Today at 12:25

Hi there,
Can you please tell me if you can give me a quote for a new piece of glass for my drawer. I'm such a bimbo I have yet again got my DIY kit out and thought I would just tighten up the handles then I heard this bloody awful ice cracking sound I've caused destruction yet again!!! Think it's time to take up knitting 😊 and put my tools on eBay!

Many thanks

• 16 July 2017 •

So it's Sunday again. I have not managed to go too far today. I only clocked 1.3km. I had to come back and catch up on some sleep after last night's antics. I bet you are all thinking, crazy kitten well no, I think it's thanks to crazy mum. Have I ever mentioned my mum can't drink? She only has to sniff a cork and she's over the limit, well as she had a slightly clumsy week she thought she might open a bottle of wine she had in the fridge, BIG MISTAKE!!! She was really pushing it as she never even bothered to mix it with soda.

Firstly, NEVER attempt to fake tan when under the influence of alcohol. she has been muttering this under her breath all morning, stating it should be written on the bottle, I'm guessing that's because she has one orange foot and one not so orange foot, two white legs, a half done tummy, half done arms. In a nutshell, she messed up big time and is starting again when she feels better today.

Secondly as myself, Faith, Gherkin and the Crazy One were very happily going off to sleep last night on her bed, time being 12.40am, yes, am. Mum was watching Top of the Pops Boybands and suddenly from nowhere my crazy mum is up on the bed dancing and singing to YMCA in that ridiculous penguin onesie. Then the crazy kitten was jumping around on her back legs like a puppy dog wondering what her tipsy mum is doing making mad shapes with her arms. While myself, Faith and Gherkin are all just giving looks of disgust that our mum could be doing this at stupid O'clock at night and starting the kitten off again. How her beautiful chandelier that sits over her bed is not broken after her knocking it umpteen times is beyond me.

She was very quiet this morning when I got back from my very short adventure. I think she is a little ashamed of herself!! I will make her suffer, but for now I need to go and catch up on some beauty sleep.
Have a Puuurfect day Peeps
Spritzer Abrahams

• 18 July 2017 •

So I've been feeling rather smug all day. As you will notice there is no map of my adventure today as yesterday when I got home I had something to eat and where as I would usually go to sleep until late in to the evening I decided to do a Houdini and I escaped out the house without her even noticing. She had workmen in and visitors over. So last night she went on a hunt around the cottage with the tracker to put it on me, I bet that funny, unprintable language was sprouting out her mouth. By then I had already been running around "MY FIELD" for hours sniggering to myself knowing that would be another night she would not sleep properly, being a stress head. Yet I felt so free and if I wanted to go and visit any of my friends around the units at the hospital for once, she would never know!!!

I knew I had to make the most of it because, yes guys you all know the saying by now, my poor ears were so going to bleed when I did decide to rock up back at the cottage and boy did she go on and on and on...."don't think you are ever going out without your tracker on again, young lady. Why do you insist on stressing me out young lady? Who do you think you are, Houdini Abrahams? "And on and on and on......I'm a cat, talk to me in cat mum and I might have a clue what you are saying to me, and lower the decibels a bit, cats have sensitive ears woman!!!

So while being smug. I've been keeping out the way to let my ears recover, but she has just put the tracker on me earlier than usual, I guess to prove a point but I'm not sure I can be bothered to go out tonight now. Think I might sleep right in the middle of her bed just to be awkward.
Will update you all soon.
Spritzer Abrahams

• 22 July 2017 •

It's been a strange old week. It was exactly a year since we lost out gorgeous sister Gizmo, so mum got a lovely candle in her memory, we all felt obliged to be on our best behaviour because obviously mum was a little more delicate this week due to this very sensitive issue!!! Yeah right, I think we behaved for all of five minutes. We decided between us it was best to keep things as normal as possible, so the crazy kitten was smashing an ornament at four am while chasing the biggest moth ever seen in Bury. Mum wondered what was going on, jumped out of bed and finally caught it on the small chandelier in the cat's bedroom with the Crazy One in tow. Mum spoilt her fun, cleaned up the mess, fed us all then headed back to bed for a few extra hours of sleep.

I've had some great adventures this week 2.6km today being my longest. She has permanently had the camera in my face though. I sleep, the camera clicks, I eat, the camera clicks. I sit next to her, the camera clicks, so I lunged yesterday, guess what? She never clicked, she BLED!!!

Last night Faith and the Crazy One decided to have a game of chase around the lounge, it got kind of loopy, both the same colour, mum getting on a bit, so telling the wrong one off when they jumped on the coffee table and knocked the photos over. I found it all very amusing, how the vase full of sun flowers remained standing is beyond me. They were lunatics, and the more she asked them to stop the worse they got. She kept saying "I remember when I owned a home"

Today the cottage was painted outside in the colour she has wanted for so long. She doesn't do the usual white, she likes "different" I've sat watching all day from my hammock, recharging for my adventure tonight. So tomorrow when I return I'm now looking for the dark cottage, can't really miss it.
So I will wish you all a Puuurrrfect evening and catch you all soon
Spritzer Abrahams

• 23 July 2017 •

Was I going to blog today? No, so why am I blogging you may ask? Because I now have something to tell you. This morning I came home from my 2.4km adventure to find mum in the shower, the usual Sunday colour now of Orange!!! Yes, yet again something had gone wrong. She had slept on her hand this time and nothing she tried was going to bring the colour off, so she was either going to have to walk around pretending she was a big fan of Michael Jackson and wear one glove, or just accept for the next three days at least she either did not leave the cottage, or if she did, she kept her hands in her pockets.

I've decided I'm willing to forgo my next few days Felix pouches, to pay for her to get a professional spray tan, so I can have one Sunday where I don't have to listen to her complaining that she is sick of being tangoed.

But that is not my main story, oh no. She just got the WOK out and let me tell you it was not pleasant!!! Everyone asleep downstairs evacuated, I had to stick it out in the hammock just to write this blog but my chest is now bad! The smoke she creates when she cooks is second to none but what she creates is not describable!! I know it started with eggs because the Crazy One had never seen one before and thought it would be fun to play football with the first one, so that ended up smashed on the floor, so the next two eggs she put in the bowl while she got organised. The Crazy One didn't find football quite as much fun in the bowl. Seriously it looked terrible, I'm lucky I'm a cat, if I was her child I would have had to be removed by social services, I would never be fed properly!! I've never seen the others move into the garden so fast as they do when that wok comes out. When the fog lifts I will holler to let them know it's safe to return but for now I'm going to keep taking short, sharp breaths and recharge for my next adventure.

So catch you all soon Peeps. Delia Smith eat your heart out!!!
Spritzer Abrahams

• 25 July 2017 •

I came back this morning after a 1.9km adventure. I had to give mummy loves to get my lunch today. I had to get out the cottage last night it turned into utter bedlam. Let me set the scene for you. One minute we were all happily watching the last episode of love island in a darkened lounge, when just as the winner was about to be announced the Crazy One comes trotting through the lounge with the biggest mouse hanging out her mouth, tail hanging down, dragging on the floor. Well mum jumped up so fast that poor Mini-Moo who had been curled up on her knee flew in the air. Munchkin now knew the chase was on so took off with the mouse, with mum close behind, screaming at her to "get out", yeah right, like that was going to work!! Myself, Mini, Justice and Tink sat downstairs listening to the chase going on upstairs. "I mean it Munchkin, get outside now, you don't bring things inside " That was the clean version, not that the Crazy One cared, she only speaks cat, and having mum chasing her around the cottage is all just one big game to her and it took ages to get them both back downstairs. She then missed the end of her programme, weeks she had sat through that rubbish and had missed the very end!! I just remember seeing the kitten fly back through the lounge towards the garden with the mouse still in her mouth and mum close behind, then all went quiet.Mum sat back down, thinking all was now sorted when Faith strolled in and started sniffing under the big water bowl. Mum thought she better go and check and to her disbelief the Crazy One had somehow hidden the mouse there. After clearing it into the bin it was time to give up watching a full programme so time for me to make a short, sharp exit and mum went to bed.

But before I left, just to keep her on her toes, I decided I wanted to play chase. It had been a while since I've been stubborn when it's come time to put my tracker on, so as soon as I saw her getting it ready I took off up the stairs and the fun began again. Well after lots of growling from me and strange language from mum, she won. I'm all ready now for a night of fun.
Catch you all soon Peeps.
Spritzer Abrahams

• 31 July 2017 •

Boy am I in trouble again folks!!! She comes waltzing in after leaving us all day to look me straight in the eye and tell me "visiting inside the mental health unit has to stop and it has to stop NOW!! " This blinking thing I wear around my neck is driving me crazy, it knows my every move, I can't hide, I can't have any secret friends or hiding places. She haunts me. NO. She stalks me, wherever she is, she stalks me!!! I would not mind, I went visiting my friends, as I thought she left me, as she left this morning with that much baggage filled with her clothes, I didn't think she was coming back today. She has been up to something but I don't know what. I thought I would be glad to see her but my poor ears are still ringing from the ear bashing. I've just had a quick bite to eat, now I'm staying upstairs out the way.

She's trying to stop the Crazy One chasing a squirrel, Munchkin has never seen one before and this chase has been going on since early this morning, so before mum left, the tracker was put on her because mum had no idea where she might end up chasing it today while she was out!!! I think the squirrel might have a death wish as it keeps coming back for more. This squirrel is nearly as big as Munchkin, so it could get interesting. So while mum shouts for the Crazy One and the Crazy One chases the squirrel, I'm just going to sit here on mums bed listening to them outside and realise with a little smile on my face this family is so far from normal it's Puuurfect.

Wishing you all a great evening.

Spritzer Abrahams

77

• 3 August 2017 •

This week has been a week of smashing ornaments and chasing moths in our household!! The Crazy One is on a mission to clear this town of every moth that dares to take flight in the area, in the process destroy mums house and all ornaments that stand tall on her shelves. Why the loony cannot stay outside with them is beyond me, but she has to bring them in and let them go, then chase them around the cottage causing utter destruction.

My mum has developed Tourette Syndrome this week, it becomes very severe about the time Munchkin appears with a moth, I sit watching with Faith from the hammock, it's a prime position, you miss nothing sitting so high up. Justice just sleeps through it all with his legs over his eyes, (looking like mum when she has a migraine, only she uses her arms, not her legs, but you get me). So this week she needs to replace a cat ornament and two photo frames, that's quite a good week then I would say. I'm just wondering how much longer she will use the excuse "It's because she's a kitten." Maybe when she's still a lunatic at seven years old she will see she's never going to change!!!

I could see my mum needed mummy loves today when I got back from a 1.6km adventure, so I went overboard and kept rolling on her feet, I'm not usually that affectionate, but hearing her on the phone saying at 2am there had been yet another "INCIDENT" involving a moth and a kitten and an ornament in the cat's bedroom I felt she deserved it. I'm so glad now I sleep through the day and go and play out at night. I leave the madness and chaos behind for a few hours of sanity. When she thinks I'm in the unit to visit my friends she is so wrong. Really, I go for my weekly therapy sessions.

She's just been sneaky and put the tracker on me early, guess she is tired and worried I might sneak out if she falls asleep early, so I will wish you all a Puuurfect, moth-less evening.
Spritzer Abrahams

• 5 August 2017 •

So I have been very restless the last twenty-four hours and have been out on three different adventures. The last one I just came back from was 1.8km and there was mum in her onesie to greet me in the lane with the dreaded video going.

We have really kept her on her toes the last few days, the crazy kitten decided to upgrade from bringing moths in to bringing in a live vole and letting it go in the kitchen, leaving mum chasing it with the dustpan and brush and having another seriously bad Tourette's outbreak. She did finally catch it and put it outside the front door but unfortunately straight into the jaws of Bagel, so said vole was left as a gift for her on the new door mat the following morning.

Then last night I thought I might stay in for a change. I never learn!! It's like Piccadilly station, one after the other, one of my sisters or brothers will start banging on the bedroom window at stupid O'clock to get in. Just let her try and ignore them. Well last night she videoed Faiths tantrum when she could not get in!!! My mum is the concierge of this cat hotel and it's open twenty- four-seven!!

Today even though mum has been tired she has had to look after a projectile vomiting crazy kitten, it's taken all day but finally the Crazy One is perking up, mum on the other hand is starting to flag but she will plod on as she knows she has to get the tracker back on me when it's charged in case I decide to go off yet again, as I'm not sure I fancy another night in tonight. I get far more peace out playing in my field than in this madhouse.
So wishing you all a Puuurfect evening.
Spritzer Abrahams

• 7 August 2017 •

Oh boy, not sure what part of the county or world you all live in but did you all just hear my mum? Yes, it was my mum not an earthquake!! We've been on a chase around the cottage because for some reason I thought it might be fun to just steal her toast. She gave chase around the lounge and I finally dropped it on the kitchen floor. Well my poor ears are bleeding, all I can hear is "Spritzer, I cleaned today and now there are crumbs everywhere!!" "Spritzer, that was mummy's dinner, thank you for stealing it!" She has been moaning on and off all day, she came down after another sleepless night looking after a poorly Tinkerbella to dirty footprints all over the kitchen floor and worktops. She loves to clean so we as a gang like to make sure we leave her something worthwhile to really get her claws into.

Then this afternoon the Crazy One killed a beautiful butterfly, she doesn't mind moths dying but this butterfly was lovely, so Munchkin got it in the ear as well!! I'm now having a little sulk on the kitchen top while my ears stop ringing and debating whether to go on an early adventure and see if I can beat the 1.6km I clocked this morning while watching mum clean up out the corner of my eye.

Catch you all later Peeps.

Spritzer Abrahams

• 11 August 2017 •

I got back from a 2.1km adventure today and after I had my lunch I could see how busy mum was so I decided that was the exact time I wanted my mummy loves, so she had to stop what she was doing and give me all the affection I deserved for being so good these last few days.

The same cannot be said for the others, Tinkerbella decided to jump on the shelf in the wardrobe from the bed, so that was "Adios" to another of mums tops by the time mum had helped unhook her from said top!! and being a manic cat it was not an easy task, let me tell you!!

Then Faith and Munchkin refused to stop using the house for circuit training practice, they kept getting under mum's feet. Mum has even taken to using a plastic cup now as she is so tired of breakages. She is willing the weather to improve so they can go and use up some energy outside. Then tonight my mum went out just before we were due our evening meal. She needed a new mop bucket, she broke hers. The time kept ticking on and on but she still didn't come back, what was she doing?

When she eventually arrived back there was a bottle of wine in the bucket she purchased, so the mop bucket was now already becoming an ice bucket for her vice!!! I heard her on the phone telling someone that as she was leaving the car park, she spotted a car and the back door was left open so she refused to leave it until she found out who it belonged to. She had tannoy announcements put out in store, to no avail so just sat there and finally the owner returned. The woman never even realised it had been left open and was so grateful she gave mum a bottle of wine to say thank you. Well that can only mean one thing!!! Crazy stupid O'clock dancing on the bed in a onesie coming up in the not too distant future when she has sniffed the cork!!!

Well finally we all got fed and I'm now fully charged, both food and tracker wise so I will wish you all a Puuurrrfect weekend.
Spritzer Abrahams

• 16 August 2017 •

I've just got back from a 1.8km adventure. Mum has been watching me like a hawk because I decided to eat another foreign body the other day. She tore a very long piece of cotton from a sock she was wearing while I was sat next to her and I decided to eat it!! I have a terrible habit of eating everything I'm not meant to; the vet finds it very strange every time my tummy has been emptied. I seem to have survived yet again, so she can stop with the worrying now!!

But there was a new ear bashing yesterday after she checked my maps. I veered away from my regular route, way into the hospital grounds, I did a big loop of the building and clocked 2.5km in the process, I thought she might be a tiny bit impressed with me, but no, I have to stick to the woodland and the fields if I don't want my ears ringing for hours after my return. I just fancied a little change of scenery. I went back to my regular route today, anything for a bit of peace!!

Talking of peace, my brother Bagel has totally lost his voice, two whole days now of pure silence. BLISS!!

Then this morning the sound that broke the silence was Munchkin hitting the floor. She must have been in a precarious place on the bed when mum threw back the duvet to get up and all I remember seeing was her flying through the air in slow motion and landing on the floor. Mum didn't mean to laugh but it was funny and the look on the Crazy Ones face as if to say "what just happened to me?" Mum ended up over snuggling her which she hates, so she was soon recovered and trying to escape her clutches.

I'm now having a very chilled out afternoon sat with my mum.
Spritzer Abrahams

• 17 August 2017 •

So last night I ventured out in the middle of that mad lightning storm. Mum tried to keep me in, but for me the comparison of the constant live checks on the tracker means I have no fear of lightning, as I'm constantly lit up at night, and that thunder was so loud, but if you have ever heard my mum shout, then there was absolutely no difference to my ears ringing outside as to me staying indoors and listening to her going on at the crazy kitten for running a million miles an hour into the kitchen, jumping onto the side of the sink, knocking the glass sitting by the side of the sink into the sink and smashing it!! Then deciding it was best not to hang around and belting it straight back outside.

For my mum who has an obsession for needing all her glasses and pots to be full sets, or having to replace them, it is becoming quite an expensive problem.

I'm not sure if I heard right, but I'm sure I heard mum say the Crazy One might need to go in therapy or maybe she said she needed therapy.

I did hear mum telling someone on the phone this morning though what a softy the Crazy One was during the storm. Really scared, lying in mums bed with her. Strange really, she spends all day knocking the living daylights out of all of us, but goes running to mum when there is a thunder storm. I suppose it was her first major one though, but just shows who is the real tough cookie of the household, "MOI" I played out in it!! I clocked 2.2km in that storm, before I decided to turn back and get dried off........

I'm now just having a nice relaxed evening watching the Crazy One chasing poor Gherkin every time she tries to come in the lounge totally ignoring mum when she tells her to stop it!!
Catch you all soon Peeps
Spritzer Abrahams

• 18 August 2017 •

Well what an evening, I've had to come and sit on the stairs out the way. Mum had two friends in for a chippy dinner. She actually offered to cook for them when she made the invite last night. That went down like a lead balloon, it was takeaway food or no food, thank you very much!! They had heard all about her cooking skills. Well because takeaway food does not really ever come in this house, Tinkerbella, Gherkin and the Crazy One were not really on their best behaviour. Jumping on coffee tables and couches and showing a bit too much interest in the fish on everyone's plates. I wouldn't mind, they got a bowl full at the end, but staring out the poor guests while they were trying to eat dinner is not very polite is it? I found it rather laughable mum saying she had been in the gym today so she could devour that meal. She eats rubbish everyday but doesn't go to the gym daily!!! Then mums friend set the printer back up and within thirty seconds the crazy one had her head deeply embedded inside said printer. What is it with her? She has always had a fascination with that thing!! Mum had to tell her to remove her head so they could get it properly set up and use it.

It must confuse the little one to see mum being sensible one minute but this afternoon witness her on a cleaning mission. (You know how it is having guests in) We caught her hoovering our double bed, yes, actually stood on the bed hoovering it, upright. She had given up with the brown tape and decided to see if it would work hoovering the bedding. If it all went wrong, then she wouldn't do it again. It actually worked a treat and she can't believe she has never tried it before. She really is one on her own!! It didn't look very stable, I sometimes wonder how she has any right to call the crazy one, "The Crazy One".

Mums friends have gone now and I'm just lying here watching Munchkin bringing in the third moth of the evening. The lounge carpet is filling up with them nicely.
I will venture off soon and wish you all a Puuurrrfect weekend.
Spritzer Abrahams

• 22 August 2017 •

Well it's been another eventful few days in our madhouse. From Tinkerbella stealing a pot of yoghurt and acting like she had done nothing wrong, although the evidence was clearly written all over her face, head and whiskers. To the crazy kitten deciding her new hang out was on the fish tank in the lounge, which has a very unstable plastic lid with a large gap, that her paws could very easily slip through!! But does she care? Not a bit, in fact she completely ignores mum when she tells her to get down. She will be in the tank by the end of the week, maybe she will learn once it all goes wrong.

Myself, being the angel of the household at the moment, I have been on some really long adventures. So mum buying me a new, cosy bed is very much appreciated for when I get home, to climb into and recharge. She also got the crazy one a new bed but hers looks like a monster. I can't think why???

I have clocked 2km this morning on my adventures and mum managed to video me finding a new way back over the neighbour's fence. Now the dogs live a few doors up I had to find another way home at the back. It took a bit of working out but I've managed it now. So I've had my lunch and now I'm all snuggled up watching the crazy one launching herself at the windows trying to catch flies.

Have a great day Peeps.

Spritzer Abrahams

• 25 August 2017 •

It's been fun and games again at Chez Abrahams.

Mum seems to have totally lost control now of the crazy one, I believe all hope is lost!! Munchkin runs this house and that's how it is, take it or leave it!! Last night while getting herself organised to go and paper collar a kitten she had recently spotted, she thought she would take the cake with her she got while out to lunch with her good friend, as she knew it could be a long time waiting around in the car. She turned her back for five minutes, came back to the kitchen and the cake was trashed. Munchkin had helped herself and what a mess she made, she had clearly enjoyed herself, the little monkey. If any of the older cats had done that, I'm sure mums Tourette's would have broken out!!

The other evening mum decided to go for a late swim, I was sat in my hammock waiting for my late meal, wondering where she had got to. Time kept ticking on. Finally, she came back and she was telling the neighbour how Justice has a new hunting place at the top of the hill on the lane and refused to move for her to pass with the car, so she had sat there and filmed him on his hunt. I'm not being funny but don't cars have horns!!! My poor tummy was starving and yet again another of my brothers from another mother was running the show!!!

I did worry her today, someone turned the tracker off. It definitely happened at the unit. I had clocked 2.2km up to that point, then it lost all satellite reception. I can just imagine her trying to stay calm. I was very good though and I did get myself home in time for lunch. I came banging at the door with the tracker and she took the collar straight off me to check it. I've had the lecture about staying away from strangers, only they are my friends now, not strangers. I'm just going to stay up in my hammock out of her way for today. I think we are all driving her a bit round the twist!! and my ears need to heal.

Have a great day Peeps.

Spritzer Abrahams

• 27 August 2027 •

Yesterday I clocked 2.4km while on my adventure and got back to a very quiet house. Mum was having a chilled afternoon after a brain scan. Not really sure what that was all about, as not sure they were likely to find anything however hard they looked!!

Then just as we were getting ready to be fed the fire service rocked up!! Don't panic, she was having the smoke alarms checked, she had actually worn them out!! It's her cooking skills, they are that good, they are guaranteed to go off almost every time she steps foot near the oven or hob.

I also nearly had a heart attack, after the new smoke alarm for upstairs was dropped, causing it to fall down the stairs, breaking on the kitchen floor.

Then they were happily giving mum the lecture about leaving the house if there was a fire, when they suddenly bolted, after having an emergency call come through on their radio!!! It all happens in my cottage, all very exciting.

We all finally got fed and she snuck the tracker back on me and got a really cute photo, though I do say so myself. Then she breaks the news to me, I am now back with an agency, myself and Munchkin. I looked at her as if to say, I might not want to be a model anymore mum, I'm a blogger now, but she went on to tell me, that she, herself had also been taken on after many years of being poorly. I will attempt to steal a couple of her new pictures to show you as its nice not to see her in that blinking onesie for a change, although she's back in it today. Watch this space. There are no half measures with my mum.

Even bigger news, my blogs are being published into a book. I will keep you all updated.
Wishing you all a Purrfect Bank Holiday
Spritzer Abrahams

• 31 August 2017 •

I thought I might have a quiet evening tonight sat in my hammock. Who am I kidding? The minute I saw her approach the oven with the little apple pie the kind neighbour made her I knew it would end in disaster!! Who forgets they put something in the oven? I awaken to the kitchen stinking yet again of the aroma of au d'cremation and she's wafting the tea towel over the smoke alarm like a woman possessed.

I think back to last night lying quietly in the lounge when suddenly the crazy one tipped the place upside down after going on the rampage after getting herself stuck in an electrical cable. How my mum has the audacity to question why the crazy one is the way she is when she cannot even be trusted to heat something up in an oven is beyond me!!

I'm a cat and can work out that when you smell burning, you would take a wild guess it's time to remove food from the oven. If still not sure, once the piercing sound of the alarm sounds, the food is definitely over cooked, so turn the oven off please because the kitchen, the place I am trying to sleep on my hammock is getting way too hot!!

I also now realise, when I do decide to get down tonight there is going to be a standoff, as my tracker is still not back on yet and it is getting late now. There is no way she will be letting me out this cottage without it. So she will just have to wait until I decide I'm ready to come down, that will be when my poor ears have stopped ringing and the smell of burnt cooking has left my fur.

I would like just one peaceful evening where we all sit quietly snuggled up as a family, like you see in the films. No drama, but I know this is Chez Abrahams and we are in for a really long winter, filled with nothing but drama because that's the way we roll!!!
Catch you all soon Peeps.
Spritzer Abrahams

• 4 September 2017 •

This weekend turned out another expensive one for mum. While she sat watching television, she heard an almighty crash in the kitchen. The clothes horse had collapsed. That was number five this year. Faith and the Crazy One had been playing tag in it the previous night, Faith sat on the top and the loony trying to keep climbing the inside and falling out of it.

Then Saturday night, I have no idea why mum decided it was time to bring the melted wok out and try and make some fresh chips again. She ended up very poorly and it was only the next day when grandma asked her to check the date on the bag of potatoes, because mum said the chips were really soggy and soaked up all the oil that she realised the potatoes were a month out of date!! Then to top that, she used a scouring pad on the wok to clean it and has completely ruined it, so now she needs a new wok as well as nearly killing herself.

I was definitely ready for my adventure last night. I clocked 2.3km before banging on the front door to let mum know I was home. I watched her return the dish to the neighbour and lie about how nice the pie was they made her. She burnt the pie!! She couldn't eat it, and now they have said they are going to make her more!!! Great, so the smoke alarm will go off again and my poor ears will be ringing again.

It was bad enough today when mum knew that Bella and the Crazy One had caught a dragon fly. She was not happy with them. We all had bleeding ears by the time she had finished screaming at them to leave it alone.

I'm learning to stay out the way in my hammock and just watch as the rest of my family carry on acting "their kind of normal" and thoroughly entertain me.
I'm going out soon to do some proper hunting, so catch you all soon.
Spritzer Abrahams.

• 8 September 2017 •

Well my facial expression says it all. The lane has been full of workmen and machinery today and the noise has been too much!! These men have torn the lane up ready to have all new tarmac tomorrow. I came back from my 1.7km adventure just to see what all the noise was. I could hear it from my field and needed to know what I was missing back home. I kind of wish I hadn't, as the machinery was so loud we were all very freaked out, and nosey mum keep opening the door to take a peak didn't help matters. I wish she would have at least got out of her onesie before chatting away. I really don't think anyone thinks my mum has any real clothes.

As the day went on the noise levels got louder and that was my mum. Her clean house was now getting dirty. Little cat paw prints were appearing all over her spotless black floors and it wasn't going down well. Justice and Faith were getting brave and venturing out on to the now torn up dirty lane and then running back in. I was loving watching this from my hammock. How many times could mum get the mop out in one afternoon?

When the guys left and it all quietened down, I would say we managed about an hour of peace before all hell broke loose. When the crazy one flew in through the door with her first ever bird, she had a yellow tit in her mouth and ran straight up the blinking stairs with it!! Mum gave chase, finally pinning her down, still with said bird in her mouth and carried her outside and quickly closed the door. The crazy kitten didn't have the first idea what she was now meant to do with the bird and the very lucky bird flew off into the woods.

After all the noise and commotion today I'm now ready for my night time adventure. Mum has been for a swim, come back and put my tracker on and after my Dreamies I'm off for some peace and quiet.

Catch you all soon Peeps.

Spritzer Abrahams

• 18 September 2017 •

I came back after a 2.1km adventure today. Let me tell you all, I left pretty sharply last night, my mum was screaming the house down while chasing Tinkerbella around the cottage. She had a mouse in her mouth and I have no idea why she brought it in, as she should have known better. None of us older ones ever bring anything inside, I don't know if she thought because the crazy one did it she could give it a go, but my mum developed Deirdre Barlow veins in her neck and she was not happy at all. Bella had the mouse running under both beds with my hysterical mother screaming like a mad woman. I decided to make a short, sharp exit. Didn't even wait around for my Dreamies I left Tink growling at mum and mum screaming at Tink, to get the mouse outside. Poor mum had not managed any peace last night. She came in after starting my new book and then after making something to eat the Crazy One thought it would be fun to attack the boiled eggs on her plate. Munchkin thinks anything that moves is a game and she has been so spoilt, she gets away with everything!!! I came back to a much calmer household this morning, mum is a little horse and we are all having our monthly flea treatment, I guess that's revenge for upsetting her last night.

We are all lying here in the lounge. It's so quiet. It's like Chez Abrahams comes to life at night, only mum probably wishes it didn't.
So I will wish you all a great afternoon.
Spritzer Abrahams

2.1 km
18/09/2017, 08:26

• 22 September 2017 •

Not a great week at Chez Abrahams. Two visits to the vets for my mum. Bagel hurt his tail badly, which I am glad to say is now on the mend and Justice is proper poorly. He isn't eating, high temperature and upset tummy. He suffers with Lymphocytic Enteritis and the vet suspects it has flared up again. Not seen him this unwell since he was a kitten, poor lad, so he doesn't know it yet but he is back again on Monday morning.

My mum went out and left us all day yesterday, no warning, just up and out. Bags packed, had no idea if she was even coming back, my little heart dropped. She went off to film her commercial she got booked in. I wondered why she had been walking around the cottage talking to herself saying the most random things for the last week. Now it made sense. They were her lines!! I would never admit it to her but I was so pleased when she walked back in. Even if she was caked in make-up.

It didn't take her long to get back in her onesie, back to the mum I know and love.

While learning her lines and running to the vets she had managed to organised with Hills Science Food for them to send Justice a special delivery. Which was there when she got home. They have altered the food he has to eat and he won't entertain it, so they found him an older version bag and sent him his own parcel in his name. Can't say I was impressed. I'm the special cat in this house not him!!

My mum got very giddy when she saw the parcel in his name. Anyway he still won't eat.

Just in case she was planning on disappearing on us again today I took a very quick adventure this morning of 1.2km, but she has stayed with us today. So I'm now chilling on the couch before a proper adventure tonight.

So I wish you all a puurrfect weekend.

Spritzer Abrahams

• 24 September 2017 •

So after not eating for nearly 10 days, Justice finally ate just a little of his special diet for mum last night. She was practically dancing on the ceiling and that was without sniffing a cork!!

She had the chance of going out last night, which she never does to meet up with friends from her junior school but she would not leave the poorly one. I kind of wish she had, we ended up on a forty-five-minute chase around the cottage last night with her trying to get the tracker on me. She had a bowl of food and was trying to entice me out from under her bed, then I ran down the stairs and around the couch. She slammed the door so I couldn't escape, so back up the stairs we went. Now the Crazy One joined us close at mum's heels, only she was clearly far more interested in the food mum was still flying around with. The chase eventually ended in the kitchen with me yet again losing and the tracker being put on. Whilst I ate what was left in the bowl that had been used on the chase, the rest of the food was strewn all over the cottage.

I clocked 1.9km today, exactly the same mileage as yesterday, yet a completely different route. I've never done that before. Mum went out today with grandma and came back very over excited with two new onesies, one having Thumper the rabbit all over it!! She can be very embarrassing because I know she will be out to meet me in the lane after one of my adventures in that onesie in the near future.

I am just lying here in my cat bed contemplating my next move now, as mum has just come in the kitchen and taken some things out the fridge and the wok out the drawer. So for my own safety I'm signing off and climbing in my hammock out the way.
Spritzer Abrahams

• 27 September 2017 •

Another crazy week at Chez Abrahams. Between us we broke clothes horse number six. Her face was a picture when she came down to find it flat on the floor a couple of days ago. Her Tourette's kicked in again until she had picked up everything and got herself a calming cup of tea.

Justice is still not eating well so at his check-up mum mentioned he had eaten a mouse, so the vet suggested he could change his diet to frozen mice, at which point my mum nearly fainted and very politely told the vet that would not be happening on her watch, thank you very much!! So another brand of special diet is going to be tried and hopefully he won't turn his nose up at that.
I decided to play up the other night and refused to get off the fridge to have my tracker put on. I guess I'm tired of not being in the limelight and just wanted mum to video me throwing a diva tantrum, which might I say I am Puuurfect at. She had to entice me down with a bowl of food. I made her wait quite some time but the food always wins in the end.

Then yesterday poor Mini-moo ended up in the vets, that's three cats in one week, even I think that's unlucky. They do say things come in three's. My vet might begin to think my mum is a stalker. Mini has some big lump on her shoulder blade. She is almost 18 years old and as agile as a kitten.

Then the new dining room table and chairs finally arrived. Yay, great, so now the Crazy One has something to sit on to jump off and pounce on us all.

It does look good but mum is already lecturing us, telling us not to go on the glass table as we may scratch and dirty it, not to go on the white chairs as we will leave dirty paw prints. Seriously mum why did you buy this table and chairs? You will never sit at it? You might get a finger print on the glass.

I actually wished it had rained when I got back from my 2km adventure this morning. I wanted to run in and jump all over it just for a laugh to see her reaction. I bet my ears would still be bleeding now.

Oh is that rain I hear on the windows?? I will just get myself ready for an extra-long, wet adventure.
Catch you all soon.
Spritzer Abrahams

• 30 September 2017 •

It's the last day of September and I'm on my third time of being on an adventure today. Well I lie, I'm out in the pouring rain, writing my blog, looking like a drowned rat but it's the only place I can get a minute's peace at the moment. Oh and did I mention the fact I don't have my tracker on? Boy am I going to get it in the ear in the morning.

Why might you ask am I sitting under a tree in the woods in the pouring rain when I could be in a nice warm cottage? Because of Gherkin, yes, it was Gherkin's turn tonight to stupidly try and sneak a vole in, and all credit to her, it might have been deceased but it was a big one and she gave mum a circuit training workout around the cottage that was amusing until Gherkin dropped it and mum stood on it!!!barefoot!! The decibels reached a pitch none of us had ever had to tolerate before and we all belted it into the garden, only I kept running and now, here I sit under this tree, my ears, they still ring, so I will not be venturing back until daybreak.

The postman who my mum specifically gave instructions never to knock with parcels or make too much noise if he was around at our lunchtime, made such a clatter with the letterbox, it spooked Justice, who tipped over his food bowl, then all my brothers and sisters in turn panicked and ran in different directions, causing the water bowl to go over. Nobody ended up eating, it was total chaos.

All so different to yesterday. It was mum's birthday, we cleverly purchased her a basic cookery book. I don't think she was too thrilled at all, we, on the other hand found it hysterical. I even got up early and gave up my Instagram page to her. For once it was not about me, it was all about her. (That won't be happening again) can't have her and my brothers and sisters stealing my thunder.

We did have a nice quiet day though. So different to the utter madness today has been, from the moment I got back from my 1.7km jaunt this morning.

They say winters are long. I can honestly say my crazy family are in for one long, adventurous winter filled with madness..............
Spritzer Abrahams

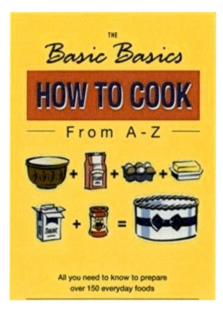

• 10 October 2017 •

It's been a few days since I've written my blog. I've been trying to stay out the way, as I've become a bit of a Houdini at escaping without my tracker on. It isn't going down very well but I'm loving not lighting up like a Christmas decoration every time she feels like live tracking me on these dark evenings. The only problem is; my ears are ringing more often when I get an ear bashing upon my return.

Talking of ear symptoms, I think everyman and his dog in Australia now has ringing ears after the way she screamed at the Crazy One last night while on yet another circuit mission of catch the cat with the mouse in her mouth!! Only when the Crazy One ran in with said mouse, mum was actually on a phone call and never hung up, so the whole crazy mission was heard by her friend, so now I have concrete proof I don't exaggerate when I say all hell breaks loose in this cottage when a mouse is brought in. To top it all, after all the running round and shouting, she only went and burnt her dinner to a cinder again. How she hadn't smelt it smouldering away is beyond me, I could smell it from the bedroom, yet she had let it, yet again get to that beautiful shade of black, only fit for the bin. After all the commotion she let us have the fish light on in our bedroom, a bit of calming time before my adventure. I also have some exciting news; my book cover was made this weekend.

Got to go now though as need to go play in my field, so have a great day.

Spritzer Abrahams

• 12 October 2017 •

OMG it's not even lunchtime and it's all happening here today. I escaped last night without my tracker, so coming back in this morning was strike number one, jumping on her white sheet with filthy paws was strike number two!!! I have this permanent buzz in my ears, I think she has caused me permanent damage, she goes on and on with herself but only speaking cat I have no idea what she is sprouting on about, I just hear this high pitched sound that really hurts. Luckily the Crazy One took the pressure off me, she kindly brought a frog in. Let me tell you. To anyone on the outside world you would have thought it was the biggest frog known to man. She screamed like a baby. In fact, it was possibly one of the tiniest frogs ever seen, but no way was she going to touch it, she had to catch it on the dustpan and brush. Not so easy as frogs have a tendency to jump!! And the crazy kitten was not giving up the frog that easily. After lots of effort and screaming she finally got it outside. Why she gave the Crazy One a lecture I have no idea, that one is never going to learn the house rules. I then decided I might like to sneak out again minus my tracker, only she clocked me and quickly locked the door, I growled and hid under the couch in the snug. Then after a long standoff and a chase around the cottage mum caught me in the bedroom. The tracker is on and now I've changed my mind. I'm staying in. To top the morning off, Tinkerbella just had her lunch then decided to throw the whole lot back up all over the lounge carpet.

I say that's one eventful morning at Chez Abrahams.

I hope you all have a great day.

Spritzer Abrahams

• 18 October 2017 •

Been a bit crazy again here at Chez Abrahams. Think I ate something that maybe I shouldn't have from the restaurant. Then the night of the big wind, I was zig zagging all over the place clocking 2.3km altogether but I was more flying through the woods and fields. I got back to utter destruction with fence panels down and all garden ornaments broken. She wasn't a happy bunny. The crazy kitten on the other hand was loving having mum outside clearing everything up, she thought it was one big game. Mum wasn't in a good mood after paying to repair all the damage. The rest of the day went pretty smoothly, until our late feed and from the corner of her eye she saw Tinkerbella sneak into the kitchen with something in her mouth. She looked closer and there was a mouse, upside down, bunny kicking, trying to escape. My mum, by now tired of us bringing gifts in flipped into Tourette's mode and screamed at her to get in the garden, and she dutifully obliged. Could things get any worse tonight? It was now very late and I was almost ready to leave for my late jaunt. Of course they could, this is Chez Abrahams, firstly mum went upstairs and realised she hadn't made up her clean bed, rotten luck. Trying to make a bed up at stupid O'clock at night!! I mean what could happen? The crazy kitten might refuse to come out from under the mattress protector sheet as per usual? Oh no, this is far more serious than that.......... Mum got the mattress protector out the linen box and was just about to shake it out when she saw the biggest, hairiest, eebyjeeby ever inside it. She can't even say the word, never mind write it. She tried to scream but nothing came out, she just stood there frozen to the spot. She needed to get downstairs to get some rubber gloves so she could touch the sheet to get it somehow into a bag. After what felt like forever and in a mad sweat, she got the sheet in to a bag and in the dustbin. She ended up staying up all night, worried maybe it had escaped. Think it's definitely time we found my mum a cat man. I'm going to think up a good write up for her, if she was to be on a dating site while out in my field later. That should entertain me for five minutes.

Catch you all soon Peeps

Spritzer Abrahams

• 20 October 2017 •

So as I promised I went off on my adventure last night, after sitting with mum while she sat doing whatever it is she is doing to try and help the cats. I never managed to go too far, only 1.1km because I decided to sit myself down and compose what I think would be the Puurrfect description of my mum, if I can get her on a dating site to find her a cat man. So here is what I have come up with:

A crazy, old lady. Partial to owning the odd cat.

Suffers from Tourette's when in close proximity to mice, eebyjeebys, frogs and voles.

Terrible O.C.D

Thinks she can do D.I.Y but ends up injured and calling in the workmen after every attempt.

Light weight in the drinking department, sniffs a cork and falls over!!

Cooking skills, none existent. But is top notch at setting off the smoke alarm!!

In my eyes, she may have flaws but she loves us to the moon and back and none of us could wish for a better mummy. So we will all have to vet (do you like that) whoever she might choose and let's see if this time next year my description of her finds us a new cat daddy. Bet my ears bleed for days when she sees this blog!!!!
P.S I have even stolen some more of her new pictures to use.

So catch you all soon I've some dating sites to check out.
Spritzer Abrahams

So this ends my first book but my blogs do not end. They continue to be written and will be published again next year. So you will be able to follow more of my adventures and see what my crazy family have been up to and of course find out did I or did I not succeed in my mission to find us a cat daddy...............

Lightning Source UK Ltd.
Milton Keynes UK
UKRC010043160119
335630UK00012B/340